HOUGHTON MIFFLIN
SOCIAL STUDIES

Contents

SUPPORT FOR LANGUAGE DEVELOPMENT

To the Teacher

If your classroom is typical of many in schools throughout the country, you have a variety of students with their own unique strengths and instructional needs. Some of your students may be struggling readers, recipients of special services, or in need of extra support to access social studies content and skills. You may have students who need to be challenged regularly. Your classroom may also have many of the increasing number of English Language Learners (ELL) who require language development and specialized teaching. *Houghton Mifflin Social Studies* addresses these subgroups of the student population and provides the resources necessary to differentiate your instruction.

Student Book includes:

- Reading Skills with Graphic Organizers that help organize information for English Language Learners and students who need extra support.

- Review questions after sections of the text that help students check their understanding.

- Hands-on and Writing Activities in Lesson Reviews to address a variety of learning styles or modalities.

- Extend Lessons for additional ways to teach important concepts through a variety of learning modalities.

- Leveled Extend Activities for extra support and challenge opportunities.

Teacher's Edition includes:

- Unit activities for Extra Support or Challenge students and English Language Learners.

- Core Lesson support for leveled instruction and strategies for teaching English Language Learners.

- Support for every Extend Lesson that includes teaching activities for all levels of learners, as well as ELL instruction.

Resources for Reaching All Learners

This booklet has three sections for meeting the needs of different types of learners:

- **Lesson Summaries** are used with Extra Support students, advanced English Language Learners, and for students who may have missed critical lessons.

- **Challenge Activities** are intended for students who can work independently on more advanced material.

- **Support for Language Development** activities address the needs of intermediate English Language Learners and other struggling learners, who might benefit from special instruction to develop their language skills.

Use with *States and Regions*

Lesson Summaries

One-page summaries highlight important concepts and details from the lessons. Each summary is written below grade level for universal access to critical social studies content. The summaries also help develop students' ability to understand the content. Before and After Reading activities direct students to circle, underline, and interact with the content as they answer review questions and identify critical vocabulary. The comprehension activities listed below can also be assigned as students read the summaries. These strategies will direct students to interact with the summary text and foster comprehension skills.

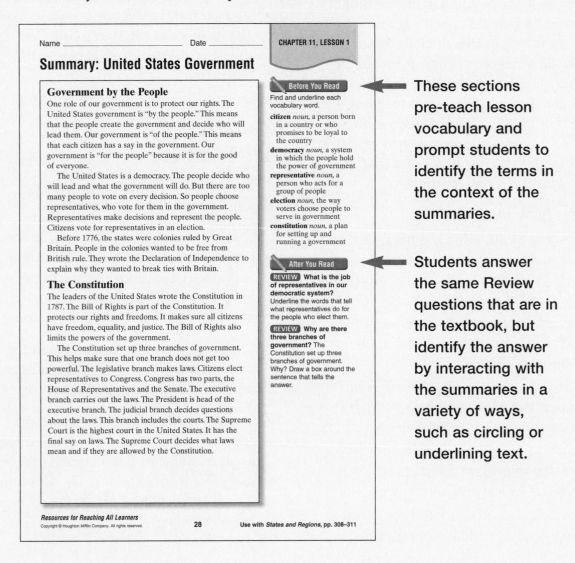

Name _____ Date _____

CHAPTER 11, LESSON 1

Summary: United States Government

Government by the People

One role of our government is to protect our rights. The United States government is "by the people." This means that the people create the government and decide who will lead them. Our government is "of the people." This means that each citizen has a say in the government. Our government is "for the people" because it is for the good of everyone.

The United States is a democracy. The people decide who will lead and what the government will do. But there are too many people to vote on every decision. So people choose representatives, who vote for them in the government. Representatives make decisions and represent the people. Citizens vote for representatives in an election.

Before 1776, the states were colonies ruled by Great Britain. People in the colonies wanted to be free from British rule. They wrote the Declaration of Independence to explain why they wanted to break ties with Britain.

The Constitution

The leaders of the United States wrote the Constitution in 1787. The Bill of Rights is part of the Constitution. It protects our rights and freedoms. It makes sure all citizens have freedom, equality, and justice. The Bill of Rights also limits the powers of the government.

The Constitution set up three branches of government. This helps make sure that one branch does not get too powerful. The legislative branch makes laws. Citizens elect representatives to Congress. Congress has two parts, the House of Representatives and the Senate. The executive branch carries out the laws. The President is head of the executive branch. The judicial branch decides questions about the laws. This branch includes the courts. The Supreme Court is the highest court in the United States. It has the final say on laws. The Supreme Court decides what laws mean and if they are allowed by the Constitution.

Before You Read
Find and underline each vocabulary word.

citizen *noun*, a person born in a country or who promises to be loyal to the country

democracy *noun*, a system in which the people hold the power of government

representative *noun*, a person who acts for a group of people

election *noun*, the way voters choose people to serve in government

constitution *noun*, a plan for setting up and running a government

After You Read

REVIEW What is the job of representatives in our democratic system? Underline the words that tell what representatives do for the people who elect them.

REVIEW Why are there three branches of government? The Constitution set up three branches of government. Why? Draw a box around the sentence that tells the answer.

Resources for Reaching All Learners
28 Use with *States and Regions*, pp. 308–311

These sections pre-teach lesson vocabulary and prompt students to identify the terms in the context of the summaries.

Students answer the same Review questions that are in the textbook, but identify the answer by interacting with the summaries in a variety of ways, such as circling or underlining text.

As You Read Comprehension Activities

The lesson summaries can also be used to reinforce students' comprehension skills. A variety of comprehension activities can be assigned to students as they read the summaries. Some of these activities include:

- **Main Idea/Details** As students read the summaries, encourage them to circle the Main Idea of each section. After they identify the Main Idea, prompt students to review the summary and locate and number the supporting details.

- **Cause and Effect** Direct students to read the summaries and analyze them for cause-and-effect statements. Once students find these statements, prompt them to organize the information in a graphic organizer.

- **Compare and Contrast** While students are reading the summaries, prompt them to locate comparing and contrasting statements. Have students record these statements in graphic organizers or on a separate sheet of paper.

- **Sequence** Begin by having students read the entire summary. Encourage students to review the summary a second time and focus on the order in which certain events are described. Then have them identify the sequence by numbering the events in the summary text. Students can also use the Sequence Chart in the Grade Level Resources to organize their answers.

Using the Lesson Summaries

- **Build background** You can give summaries to students before teaching the Core Lesson. Use the summaries as background with the whole class, as part of a reading group, with individualized instruction, or as homework in place of reading the Core Lesson itself. The summaries provide students with the critical lesson information (lesson content and structure) they need to participate in class discussions.

- **Reinforce concepts** After teaching the Core Lesson, you may distribute the summaries to students to ensure their thorough understanding and to offer lesson reinforcement.

- **Reteach the Core Lesson** After assessing students' understanding of the lesson content, you may find the need to reteach some or all of the content to students. The summaries provide a more interactive opportunity to absorb the concepts so that all students will be prepared for chapter-level assessment.

- **Assess Extra Support students in a real and fair way.** Each summary includes all the information needed to answer the Core Lesson Review questions, so the informal, continuous assessment of classroom comprehension checks can be applied to Extra Support students. Lesson Tests, provided in the *Assessment Options* booklet that comes with your program, have been written so that students who have only read the Lesson Summaries can answer them. They can therefore be used with the entire class.

Challenge Activities

These activities—two or three per chapter—are intended for students who show their understanding of the material and are ready to be challenged with independent work that develops research, writing, and other skills. Assign Challenge activities to those students for whom a particular chapter or unit is more easily mastered. Additionally, some of these activities may also work well, perhaps with some support, with English Language Learners who demonstrate conceptual understanding.

Using the Challenge Activities

These activities are for independent work. You can copy the page and let students choose which activity they are interested in completing. You can also cut the page into smaller, individual activity sheets and assign them to students based on the skills that they need to develop.

Support for Language Development

English Language Learner Support

A growing number of English Language Learners no longer have the option of waiting to master the language prior to learning content area concepts and skills. The challenge in teaching social studies to these students is to deliver the content without diluting it. The goal of ELL support is to provide *universal access to the content through differentiated paths.*

- Much of the ELL student's need is to have the abstract made concrete.

- In working with ELL students in a mainstreamed classroom, begin with instruction to all students, and then provide scaffolding to those who require additional support.

- The ELL student progresses best with adult interaction. Therefore interactive teacher support suggestions are provided.

- Good teaching—interactive, multilayered, varied—is good for all students but is *essential* for students who are learning English.

English Language Learners and *Houghton Mifflin Social Studies*

If you have English Language Learners in your classroom, you are aware that ELL students are not a monolithic group with one set of skills. Students may be at Beginning, Intermediate, and Advanced levels of language acquisition. These levels can be described in a variety of ways. In *Houghton Mifflin Social Studies,* this simple system is used to describe the different levels:

- **Beginning** students are at the earliest stage of English language acquisition and may have a much greater ability to understand English than to speak it. This is sometimes called *preproduction* or *early production.* Many of the strategies suggested in the Teacher's Edition focus on Beginning students. Beginning students should be paired with an aide, or other more English-proficient students who speak their native language, if they are to successfully use the Support for Language Development materials in this booklet.

- **Intermediate** students are more able to comprehend and express themselves in English. This group is called *speech emergent* for that reason. The Teacher's Edition includes strategies for the Intermediate group. The Support for Language Development materials in this booklet were designed so that students can use the pages independently or with limited help.

- **Advanced** students are in the final stages of becoming fluent speakers and can be considered *transitioning* or having acquired *intermediate fluency*. This group works more independently and might help beginning students with the Support for Language Development activities in this booklet. There are advanced ELL strategies in the Teacher's Edition, and many of the Extra Support strategies can be useful. In addition, Advanced ELL students have reached the level where the Lesson Summaries in this booklet would be excellent support.

For native English-speaking students with weak vocabulary and verbal skills, use the Support for Language Development activities. These activities employ non-verbal/visual instructional strategies (i.e. visual presentations and expressions) in a variety of formats that reinforce critical social studies content. ELL students may benefit from these strategies, along with the visual approach to vocabulary instruction.

Using the Support for Language Development

The Support for Language Development worksheets can be used in these ways: for independent work, to provide limited support for intermediate English language learners, and to provide more support for Beginning students. For each lesson, students are supported in two essential areas:

- **Vocabulary**
- **Tested Objectives**

Vocabulary The social studies vocabulary taught in each lesson of *Houghton Mifflin Social Studies* identifies key concepts in the areas of History, Geography, Economics, Citizenship, and Culture. Students, especially second language learners, may find some terms to be unfamiliar. Houghton Mifflin's approach to critical vocabulary is through the use of visual strategies. All vocabulary words are pictured on the pages, and students reinforce their understanding of them by connecting the words, the visuals, and their meanings in a variety of ways. You can use these worksheets to create an illustrated glossary that students may refer to as they develop their language skills.

Tested Objectives This section covers one or more of the lesson's tested objectives and enables students to focus on the most relevant factual matter and the most important ideas in the lesson. Students will complete a variety of activities that include fill-in-the-blanks, directed questions, and graphic organizers that help in the acquisition and connection of information.

Summary: The Geography of Our World

Welcome to Geography

Geography is the study of the people and places of Earth. It explains forces that shape the land. Geographers study how our environment affects us and how we affect our environment. Geographers ask three questions about a place. They ask, "Where is it?" If you want to tell someone where you live, you can say your address or you can say where your home is in relation to other places. Geographers ask, "Why is it there?" They look for clues about forces that shaped mountains, rivers, landforms, and bodies of water.

Geographers study why some communities grow and some disappear. They ask "What is it like there?" They study the physical features of the land. They also study human features, such as how people use land, the work they do, their foods, languages, and beliefs.

Where in the World Are You?

A globe shows the earth's oceans and continents. Continents are masses of land. There are four large oceans: the Atlantic, Arctic, Pacific, and Indian. There are seven continents: Africa, Antarctica, Asia, Australia, Europe, North America, and South America. The earth can be divided into hemispheres. The United States is in the Northern and Western Hemispheres. The United States has many regions. A region is an area that can be described by features, such as the language people speak there or the kinds of landforms found there.

Maps with latitude and longitude lines show the exact location of a place. Latitude lines run parallel to the equator. Lines of longitude, also called meridians, run from the North Pole to the South Pole. The lines have numbers, called degrees. The equator is 0 degrees latitude. It divides Earth into two hemispheres, Northern and Southern. Other latitude lines are measured in degrees north or south. The prime meridian is 0 degrees longitude. Other longitude lines are measured in degrees east or west. To give the exact location of a place, find where the latitude and longitude lines cross. For example, New Orleans is at 30 degrees north, 90 degrees west. This is written as 30° N, 90° W.

Before You Read

Find and underline each vocabulary word.

geography *noun,* the study of the people and places of Earth

environment *noun,* all the surroundings and conditions that affect living things

hemisphere *noun,* one half of the earth's surface

region *noun,* an area that is defined by certain features

After You Read

REVIEW What are two ways to describe the location of a place? Highlight the sentence that tells how you can describe where you live.

REVIEW What physical features does a globe show? Draw a box around the sentence that tells what features are shown on a globe.

REVIEW Why are maps useful? What does a map with latitude and longitude lines show? Underline the sentence that tells the answer.

Resources for Reaching All Learners
1
Use with *States and Regions*, pp. 6–11

Summary: Land and Water

Major Landforms

Natural forces shape and change the earth. Some natural forces take place underground. Slowly moving tectonic plates cause earthquakes and volcanoes . Melted rock from volcanoes can form mountains. Volcanoes created the Cascade Mountains in the northwest United States. The Rocky Mountains in the western part of North America were formed when tectonic plates pushed together. The tectonic plates broke and moved rocks deep in the earth's crust.

Land is also shaped by erosion . Wind and water carve valleys and deep canyons in rock. Wind can also blow soil away. Erosion rounded the Appalachian Mountains that run from Maine to Alabama in the eastern United States. Glaciers once covered parts of North America. They pushed soil and rocks as they moved. Moving glaciers also caused erosion. They helped shape hills, valleys, and plains.

Bodies of Water

Moving glaciers scooped soil and rocks to form basins. When the glaciers melted, some water stayed in these basins. This is how the five Great Lakes were created.

Lakes form when water enters a low area faster than it can leave. Some lakes drain out through rivers. Some water seeps into the ground. Some water evaporates into the air. The only way water can leave Utah's Great Salt Lake is by evaporating. Minerals left behind make the water salty.

Rivers form as water moves over high land to lower land. Small streams flow into larger ones. Larger streams flow into rivers. Rivers flow into the ocean. The Mississippi River is the longest in North America. It starts in Minnesota and drains into the Gulf of Mexico. Many other rivers flow into the Mississippi. The Mississippi is one of the world's busiest shipping routes.

People have always settled near rivers. Rivers bring water for drinking and farming. Rivers provide transportation. Flowing water runs machines.

Before You Read

Find and underline each vocabulary word.

tectonic plate *noun,* a huge slab of slowly moving rock beneath the earth's crust

erosion *noun,* a process of wearing away rock and soil

glacier *noun,* a huge mass of slowly moving ice

basin *noun,* an area with a low center surrounded by higher land

After You Read

REVIEW **What forces can shape the land?** Highlight six forces that can shape the land.

REVIEW **In what way did glaciers create the Great Lakes?** As glaciers moved, they scooped up soil and rocks. What did this create? Draw a box around the paragraph that tells the answer.

---

2 Use with *States and Regions,* pp. 16–19

Summary: Resources of the United States

A Land of Rich Resources

Natural resources are things from the natural environment that people use. The first Americans used natural resources, such as water, soil, plants, and animals. Food, clothing, houses, and fuel all come from natural resources. Trees and other living things are renewable resources. Soil is renewable if it is used carefully. Minerals like copper and iron are nonrenewable resources. They were formed over millions of years. Once we use them up, they will be gone forever. Sunlight, wind, and water are flow resources. We can use their energy as they move through the environment.

Using Natural Resources

Rich soil covers much of the land in the United States. People use soil to raise crops and livestock. There are great forests in North America. People cut trees to make wood and paper products. The oceans are a source of seafood. Rivers provide transportation routes and their flow generates power. We use water for drinking and farming.

Miners dig for mineral resources, such as metals and stone. People use natural resources to make energy. We use energy for electricity, heat, and transportation. Most of our energy comes from burning fossil fuels, such as coal, oil, and natural gas. The United States produces much of the world's fossil fuels. It also uses more fuel than any other country. Fossil fuels are nonrenewable resources.

Using Resources Wisely

People are finding other energy resources. The sun's power and heat from within the earth are used to make energy. Wind and water are used to make electricity. Nuclear energy uses natural resources, but it causes safety problems.

People do not always use natural resources wisely. People dump waste into water, burn fuels that harm the air, cut too many trees, and take too many fish. You can help to protect natural resources by using less energy and recycling.

Before You Read

Find and underline each vocabulary word.

natural resources *noun,* things from the natural environment that people use

renewable resources *noun,* things that the environment can replace after we use them

nonrenewable resources *noun,* things nature cannot replace after we use them

product *noun,* something that is made from natural resources

fossil fuel *noun,* an energy source formed by the remains of things that lived long ago

After You Read

REVIEW **What is a natural resource?** Highlight the sentence that tells the answer.

REVIEW **Why are natural resources important to the people of the United States?** Highlight ways that people in the United States use natural resources.

REVIEW **How can you help protect natural resources?** Circle the sentence that tells what you can do to protect natural resources.

Summary: What Is a Region?

Defining Regions

The world can be divided into regions. A region is an area that shares one or more features. These features make regions different from one another. People use regions to organize their ideas about places and people. For example, a farming region is different from a fishing region. A farming region in Europe may grow different crops than a farming region in Asia.

Countries and states are regions that have the same government. Other regions are based on landforms or the plants or animals that live there. Regions can be based on the population. People may share a religion or language.

Regions take up space or land. Some regions have borders to show exactly where they begin and end. Countries and states have borders that show exactly what land area they contain. Other regions have a boundary. Some boundaries, like rivers, are natural. Some are man-made, such as a road.

How Regions Are Used

Creating regions helps people to understand and organize large spaces. Governments divide their countries or states into regions. Government leaders gather facts about the people, environment, and natural resources in each region. They use this information to decide how to use resources and give services to people who need them.

People use regions to make decisions. Business leaders use information about regions to decide if they want to open a store or sell a product there. For example, a company that makes coats looks for regions with cold weather.

Regions can overlap. The same place can be in more than one region. For example, the city of Elizabeth is in the state of New Jersey. It is also in the New York metropolitan region, because it is close to that city. It is also in the East, a region of the United States.

Before You Read

Find and underline each vocabulary word.

government *noun*, a system of making and carrying out rules and laws

population *noun*, the people who live in an area

religion *noun*, a system of faith or worship

boundary *noun*, the edge of a region

After You Read

REVIEW **What kind of region has borders?** Underline the sentence that tells which regions have borders.

REVIEW **In what ways do people use regions to make decisions?** Draw a box around two sentences that tell how the government and business leaders use regions to decide what to do.

4 **Use with *States and Regions*, pp. 36–39**

Name _____ Date _____

Summary: Regions of the United States

Types of Regions

The United States has many regions. One way people define regions is by physical features, such as landforms or water systems. The United States has mountain regions, valleys, plateaus, and plains. Other regions include wetlands, grasslands, forests, and deserts. Regions can also be defined by human features, such as religion or language. Over time, as the population changes, the region may also change. The region may grow or shrink.

Regions can also be defined by the work people do. For example, parts of Kansas are in the Wheat Belt, a region where many farmers grow wheat. The Silicon Valley in California is a region where many people work at computer jobs.

Other regions can be defined by the kinds of communities people live in. Cities are urban regions. The smaller towns around cities are called suburban. Together, cities and suburban regions are called metropolitan regions. Country areas are rural. They do not have cities or many people.

States and Regions

In this book, the United States is divided into four major regions: the East, the South, the Midwest, and the West. They are named for their geographic location. Each region includes several states that are close together. States in a region share natural features. They may have similar landforms or animals. For example, states in the West use the same rivers to water their farmland.

Human features also link the states in each region. Much of the land in the West was once controlled by Spain and Mexico. The states in the West share a common history. States in a region are also linked by their economy. In the South, agriculture and factories are important for the economy. Many people work on farms or in factories. Some regions are linked to a special feature, like a major city or favorite sports team. These ideas are a small part of what makes up a region.

Before You Read

Find and underline each vocabulary word.

urban *adjective,* in a city

suburban *adjective,* in smaller towns near a city

rural *adjective,* in country areas with fewer people and no large cities

economy *noun,* the way the people of an area choose to use the area's resources

agriculture *noun,* the business of farming

After You Read

REVIEW **Over time, what might happen to regions that are based on human features?** Underline two sentences that tell what happens when populations change.

REVIEW **Why does each state belong to a certain region?** Draw a box around three sentences that tell how states are linked in a region.

Summary: Climate Regions

Weather and Climate

Weather is the day-to-day conditions in the atmosphere. Air movement causes weather conditions to change. Weather conditions are factors like wind speed and direction, precipitation, and temperature. Weather conditions determine the climate of a region. Climate is the usual weather conditions in a place over a long period of time.

Three things affect climate. The first is latitude. Places far from the equator get less heat from the sun and are colder. The second is distance from a big body of water. Places closer to an ocean have a smaller change in temperature between seasons. Third, the elevation of a region affects temperature.

A Land of Many Climates

The United States has six climate regions. They are based on temperature and precipitation. Tropical regions are warm all year. Hawaii is in a tropical wet subregion. Dry regions get little precipitation. The region near the Rocky Mountains is dry. The mild mid-latitude regions have hot summers and mild winters. California is in this region.

Severe mid-latitude climates in the middle of the United States have cold winters. Polar regions such as Northern Alaska are colder year-round. The highland climate region is in the mountains, which are cooler and wetter than the lower land around them.

Climate and People

Climate affects how people live. People heat or cool their houses. People in dry regions must use water carefully to have enough to drink and water crops.

Climate also affects the economy. In Maine or Alaska, the growing season is short, so people cannot farm all year long. But California has two growing seasons, and farming is very important to the economy.

Extreme weather, like hurricanes, tornadoes, and blizzards, can destroy buildings and crops. Burning fossil fuels may be changing weather patterns by warming the earth.

Before You Read

Find and underline each vocabulary word.

precipitation *noun*, water that falls to the earth as rain, snow, sleet, or hail

temperature *noun*, a measure of how hot or cold the air is

climate *noun*, the usual weather conditions in a place over a long period of time

elevation *noun*, the height of the land

After You Read

REVIEW **What causes daily changes in the weather?** Underline the sentence that tells what causes weather conditions to change.

REVIEW **What factors are used to divide the United States into climate regions and subregions?** Circle the sentence that tells what climate regions are based on.

REVIEW **In what ways are people affected by extreme weather events?** Draw a box around the sentence that tells what extreme weather does to people and their surroundings.

Name _____ Date _____

Summary: Land and Climate

Land and Water of the East

The region between the coast of the Atlantic Ocean and the Great Lakes is called the East. It includes six New England States and five Mid-Atlantic states. The East has mountains and plains. It also has many lakes and rivers.

The Appalachian Mountains stretch from Maine to Alabama. They were formed millions of years ago when two continents collided. Wind and weather wore the mountains down. Glaciers made valleys in the mountains.

The coastal plain is east of the Appalachians. In New England, the coastal plain is mostly underwater. The coastal plain is wider from Massachusetts to Florida. People built big cities, farms, and factories on the coastal plain. More people live there than in the mountains. The land is less rough and it is closer to water routes. In the mountains people farm, mine coal, and cut trees.

The East is a land of lakes, rivers, and ocean. Glaciers formed many lakes. Rocks and sand left by glaciers also formed islands and capes. People built settlements near the best bays along the coast. Ships from other continents carried people and goods into these harbors along the coast. Boats could come inland on big rivers. Some of the rivers had waterfalls. People learned to use the waterfalls to power machines.

Climate and Its Effects

The East is about halfway between the North Pole and the equator. The East's location affects its climate. The climate is temperate. It is not too cold or too hot. There are four seasons. Winters are snowy and cold. Summers are warm and humid. It rains or snows during the four seasons.

The ocean affects the coastal climate. Cool breezes blow from the sea on hot days, and warm breezes blow on cold days. The climate affects the people, animals, and plants that live there. People cope with cold winters. Animals' food supplies change with the seasons. Squirrels bury nuts to dig up in winter. Bears and other animals hibernate. They sleep for up to 100 days. Trees like maples and oaks drop their leaves each winter to survive the lack of water.

Before You Read

Find and underline each vocabulary word.

coast *noun,* land that borders an ocean

coastal plain *noun,* flat, level land next to a coast

cape *noun,* a point of land that sticks out into the water

bay *noun,* a body of water partly surrounded by land but open to the sea

temperate *adjective,* without extremes

After You Read

REVIEW **Why are more cities built on the coastal plain than in the mountains?** Circle the words that tell about land in the mountains.

REVIEW **In what ways does the climate of the East affect the people, animals, and plants that live there?** Draw a box around 6 sentences that tell what people, animals, and trees do to live in the climate.

Summary: Resources and Economy

Natural Resources of the East

People in the East use natural resources to get the things they want and to make goods to sell. People mine coal in the Appalachian Mountains. The coal is used to make electricity. Granite and marble from Maine and Vermont are used to make buildings. Forests are cut down to make houses, paper, furniture, and fuel. Many fruits and vegetables are grown in the East. Maine farmers grow blueberries and potatoes. Cranberries are grown in sandy marshes in New Jersey and Massachusetts. The Atlantic Ocean is an important resource for fish and shellfish.

Working in the East

The United States has a market economy. People can start almost any business. They can decide what to make, how to make it, and how to sell it. They keep the profit after they pay for materials, labor, and other costs. This is different than a command economy. In a command economy, the government decides what to make, who will make it, and who will get it.

People trade resources or money for goods. When people trade a lot the economy grows. Businesses use trade to get the resources they need. Moving goods is part of trade. Trucks move raw materials to factories and finshed products to stores.

Some businesses make goods, such as chemicals, medicines, machinery, and clothing. Then they sell the goods. Other businesses perform services that people want. Lawyers, plumbers, and banks sell services.

Elements of Business

Businesses use human resources and capital resources to make things. They need people, equipment, and some raw materials. These are called factors of production. Entrepreneurs use these to start and own businesses. In our market economy, we have private ownership. This means that business owners make decisions and earn profits. Individual people, not the government, own the factors of production.

Before You Read

Find and underline each vocabulary word.

market economy *noun,* a system that lets people decide what to make, buy, and sell

profit *noun,* money left over after a business pays all its expenses

factors of production *noun,* the people and materials needed to make goods or provide services

human resources *noun,* the services, knowledge, skills, and intelligence that workers provide

capital resources *noun,* the tools, machines, buildings, and other equipment a business uses to make goods or provide services

After You Read

REVIEW **Why is the farmland of the East an important natural resource?** Underline crops farmers grow in the East.

REVIEW **How is making goods different from performing services?** Draw a box around the paragraph that tells the answer.

REVIEW **Why is private ownership important in a market economy?** Circle the sentence that tells what owners of a business do.

Use with *States and Regions,* pp. 78–83

Summary: People of the East

First Peoples

American Indians have lived in the East for thousands of years. Each group's culture was affected by climate and natural resources. Indian nations used resources differently. The Haudenosaunee, who are also called the Iroquois, built houses, tools, weapons, and canoes with wood from the forests. In the north, the growing season was short, so the Micmac hunted for food. Further south, the growing season was longer. The Lenni Lenape grew corn and tobacco. They farmed in the summer and hunted in the winter. Today, American Indians in the East have a modern lifestyle, but preserve their culture.

Colonies and Traders

Explorers from Europe came to North America in the 1500s. In the 1600s, Pilgrims and Puritans came to practice their religion freely. England started colonies in the East along the coast. The Dutch settled in the Hudson River Valley. Along the St. Lawrence River, the French traded pots, cloth, and tools for furs from the Indians.

More Europeans came. They built towns and farms. They forced the Indians from most of their land. By the late 1700s, many American colonists wanted to be free from England. They fought the British and won independence. The new nation's constitution provided a written plan for the country's new government. Europeans had brought captives from Africa to the Americas and enslaved them. Most enslaved Africans worked in the South. Some traders in the East grew rich from this business of slavery. Ship building was another important business.

Factories and Workers

By the end of the 1700s, new inventions changed life for workers. A new spinning machine and power loom helped make the textile industry grow. Many young women came from farms to work in the textile industry. Cities grew as immigration increased. In the late 1800s, millions of people fled war and poverty in Europe and came to find jobs in American factories. Many African Americans also moved north to work in factories.

Before You Read

Find and underline each vocabulary word.

culture *noun,* the way of life of a particular group of people, including beliefs and values

constitution *noun,* a plan for setting up and running a government

slavery *adjective,* an unjust system in which one person owns another

industry *noun,* a business that makes goods in factories

immigration *noun,* the movement from one nation to another

After You Read

REVIEW How did climate and natural resources affect American Indian cultures in the past? Draw a box around sentences that tell how Indians lived.

REVIEW In what ways did the East change after Europeans arrived? Underline the sentence that tells how the Europeans affected the Indians who lived there.

REVIEW What caused many immigrants to come to the United States in the late 1800s? Highlight the sentence that tells why people left Europe and came to America.

Use with *States and Regions,* pp. 90–95

Summary: What's Special About New England

Where People Live

There are six states in New England: Connecticut, Maine, Massachusetts, New Hampshire, Rhode Island, and Vermont. The biggest city is Boston in Massachusetts. It has a big harbor. Boston was once a major shipping center. Now, Boston is a center for banking and insurance. There are factories that make goods and high-tech products. Publishing and printing are important industries.

In the mid-1800s, many immigrants from Ireland moved to Boston. Many Italian people came to Boston in the late 1800s. After World War I, many African Americans moved from the South to Boston. Immigrants from Europe, Asia, Latin America, and Africa have come to live in Boston and the suburbs around it. Some of these people work in the city. They have to drive to work or take the subway. Boston was the first U.S. city to build a subway.

The Puritans who founded the city created strong social institutions. They built the first free school and Harvard, the first American college. It became a university. Religion was an important subject in these schools. Puritans wanted their children to learn to read the Bible. Today, there are many schools, universities, and places of worship in Boston.

Rural New England

Rural New England includes New Hampshire, Vermont, and Maine. Most people in rural areas work in service industries, such as tourism. Some work in manufacturing. Many workers are commuters who work in nearby cities. There are farmers in New England. The soil is rocky and the growing season is short. Most New England farmers grow one crop or raise dairy cows.

Many people travel to New England for their vacations. Tourists like to visit historical places. They go skiing in the mountains or swim at the beach. Some tourists go to festivals.

Before You Read

Find and underline each vocabulary word.

suburb *noun,* a community that grows up outside of a larger city

university *noun,* a school with several colleges that each focus on one area of study

manufacturing *noun,* making goods from other materials

commuter *noun,* a person who travels between home and work every day

After You Read

REVIEW **What kinds of social institutions did the Puritans build?** Circle two social institutions that were started by the Puritans.

REVIEW **In what ways do rural New Englanders make a living?** Highlight sentences that tell about the work people who live in rural areas do.

Use with *States and Regions,* pp. 106–109

Summary: What's Special About the Mid-Atlantic Region

Find and underline each vocabulary word.

Where People Live

The Mid-Atlantic region contains New York, New Jersey, Maryland, Delaware, Pennsylvania, and Washington, D.C. There are many big cities in this region. New York City is the largest city in the nation. It was built at the mouth of the Hudson River. Ships from Europe sailed into the big harbor. European settlers used the river to move resources and goods from inland North America to Europe. Trade developed. The city spread out to include Brooklyn, Queens, Staten Island, and the Bronx. People come to New York from all over the world. New York City has skyscrapers. It is a world center for publishing, advertising, and technology. Millions of tourists visit New York every year. They enjoy museums and plays. They visit famous places like the Statue of Liberty.

Suburbs surround the cities in the Mid-Atlantic region. People moved to the suburbs because the cities became crowded. There are many farms in the Mid-Atlantic region. Farms produce dairy products, chickens, and flowers. Coal is mined in Pennsylvania. Tourists ski on the mountains and swim at the beaches. They also visit Washington, D.C., the nation's capital.

State Governments

Each state in the United States has its own constitution and government. The government is in the capital city. State governments have three branches. The legislative branch makes the laws. The executive branch makes sure the laws are put into action. The governor of the state is the head of the executive branch. The judicial branch explains the laws in courts. State governments are public institutions. They provide education, fire and police protection, and highways for people in the state. They pay for these services by collecting taxes. People can be taxed on the property they own, the purchases they make, or the money they earn.

skyscraper *noun*, a very tall building

legislative branch *noun*, the branch of government that makes the laws

executive branch *noun*, the branch of government that makes sure the laws are put into action

judicial branch *noun*, the branch of government that interprets, or explains, the laws in courts

governor *noun*, the head of the executive branch in the state government

REVIEW **Why was New York's location important to its growth?** What did European settlers use the river for? What was the result? Draw boxes around the sentences that tell you the answers.

REVIEW **What are the three branches of state government and what do they do?** Highlight the three branches of government. Underline the sentences that tell what each branch is responsible for.

Summary: Land and Climate

Land and Water of the South

There are fourteen states in the South. The region is divided into the Upper South and the Lower South. The Upper South has high flat areas called plateaus. Some states have rolling hills and rich river valleys. Some states in the Lower South are at sea level. They have beaches, swamps, and wetlands.

The coastline of the South includes both the Atlantic Ocean and the Gulf of Mexico. These coastal plains are the lowlands. The Gulf coastal plain stretches from the Rio Grande in Texas to the tip of the Florida peninsula. The Atlantic coastal plain stretches from Florida along the Atlantic Ocean to Virginia. The Appalachian Mountains and the Ozark Plateau are in the interior. They are the South's highest landforms.

The Mississippi River carries fertile soil to the huge delta at the Gulf of Mexico. There are also other wetlands in the South. Cities in the South grew near rivers or coasts. People use water to travel and move goods.

Climate and Wildlife

The South is closer to the equator and tends to be warmer and moister than northern regions. It also has a longer growing season. Southern farmers can grow crops for most of the year.

The South has more than one climate. The latitude, elevation, and closeness to the water affect climate. These factors can be different in each state. The ocean keeps temperatures in coastal areas warm. Winters can be mild and summers can be hot and humid. It is colder in the hills and plateaus. In the Ozark highlands there are often storms and tornados. Tropical storms and hurricanes cause flooding and other damage in the South every year.

Plants and animals have adapted to the Southern climate. In Florida, mangrove trees live in salty swamps. Along the coast, sea turtles hide their eggs on beaches above the high tide line.

Before You Read

Find and underline each vocabulary word.

peninsula *noun*, a piece of land surrounded by water on three sides

interior *adjective*, an area away from the coast or border

delta *noun*, a triangle-shaped area at the mouth of a river

adapt *verb*, to change in order to better fit in an environment

After You Read

REVIEW **In what ways is the Gulf coastal plain different from the Ozark Plateau?** Highlight sentences that tell about each region.

REVIEW **Why does the South have such a variety of climates?** Underline the sentence that tells about latitude and elevation.

Use with *States and Regions*, pp. 132–135

Name _____ Date _____

Summary: Resources and Economy

Production in the South

Southerners use natural resources to produce goods and services. They use water moving through dams to make electricity. Farmers grow food. People mine coal and pump oil from underground. They catch ocean fish.

Producers turn these raw materials into many different products. The products are sold to consumers. Producers can also be consumers. They often have to buy supplies before they can make their product. For instance, owners of textile mills buy raw cotton. They spin the cotton to produce cotton yarn. Other manufacturers buy the cotton yarn to make T-shirts.

A Diverse Economy

In the past, farming was the most important part of the South's economy. It is still important. Texas, North Carolina, and Georgia rank in the top ten in numbers of U.S. farm jobs. Farmers produce rice, cotton, tobacco, sugar cane, oranges, hogs, chickens, and cattle. Other Southerners work in cotton mills and textile factories. They make yarn, cloth, and carpets. In Georgia, Arkansas, and Alabama people use trees to produce lumber and paper. People in West Virginia, Kentucky, and Texas mine coal. The coal is used to create energy. Many Southerners work in ground and air transportation. Others work in the tourism, aerospace, and oil industries. The federal government is one of the biggest employers in the South.

The economy is controlled by choices businesses and consumers make. Businesses choose which products to make. They choose how much money to charge for their products. Consumers choose which products to buy. Sometimes things happen that affect those choices. Imagine a frost hurt an orange grove in Florida. The price of orange juice would go up because of scarcity. Consumers have to decide if they are willing to pay more for this product. What someone gives up to get something else is called the opportunity cost. Every economic choice has an opportunity cost.

Before You Read

Find and underline each vocabulary word.

dam *noun*, a barrier built across a waterway to control the flow and level of water

producer *noun*, someone who makes or sells goods or services

consumer *noun*, someone who buys goods and services

scarcity *noun*, when there are not enough resources to provide a product or service that people want

opportunity cost *noun*, what someone gives up to get something else

After You Read

REVIEW **What factors of production are needed to create cotton T-shirts?** Highlight sentences that tell how a T-shirt is made.

REVIEW **What choices do producers and consumers make?** Underline sentences that tell about choices.

Summary: People of the South

First Peoples in the South

Native Americans lived in the South for thousands of years before Europeans came in the 1500s. They planted crops and became skilled farmers. Europeans later grew rice and tobacco. They used the South's rich soil and warm weather. Tobacco became an important export. In 1619, the first enslaved Africans were brought to the colony of Jamestown. They were forced to work for free in the colony.

A Plantation Economy

Some Europeans started huge farms called plantations. Most plantations only grew one crop. The main crops were rice, tobacco, cotton, hemp, indigo, and sugar. Inventions helped planters reduce costs and make bigger profits.

Plantations were like small villages. The owners lived in big houses. They had fine clothing, jewels, and art. Enslaved Africans lived in rough cabins and had few belongings. Most southerners did not enslave people.

Northern states passed laws that made slavery illegal. Many southerners said their economy depended on slavery. In 1861, eleven southern states left the United States to start their own country. A Civil War between the North and South began. After four years, the South lost. Slavery was outlawed. More than 4 million African Americans were freed.

Civil Rights and Progress

One hundred years after the Civil War, African Americans still struggled for their civil rights. **Slavery had ended, but they did not have equal treatment. Many Americans worked to win equality for all people.**

In 1954, separate schools for white and black children were outlawed. Martin Luther King Jr. helped organize a bus boycott after Rosa Parks refused to give up her seat to a white person. The bus company finally agreed to treat all riders equally.

Other groups, including women, American Indians, and Latinos began to demand their civil rights. Women won the right to vote in 1920. Today, people from different backgrounds hold important positions in all areas of American life.

Before You Read

Find and underline each vocabulary word.

export *noun*, a product that is sent out of the country to be sold or traded

boycott *noun*, a protest in which people refuse to do business with a person or company

civil rights *noun*, the rights that every citizen has by law

After You Read

REVIEW **Why did farmers in the South grow tobacco and rice?** Highlight words that tell about the land and climate.

REVIEW **In what ways were the lives of plantation owners and enslaved workers different?** Circle the paragraph that tells about plantation life.

REVIEW **Why did African Americans boycott and protest in the 1950s and 1960s?** Highlight words that tell what people wanted.

14 Use with *States and Regions*, pp. 148–153

Summary: What's Special About the Upper South

Where People Live

The Upper South has six states: Kentucky, Tennessee, Virginia, Arkansas, North Carolina, and West Virginia. Much of the land is rural and forested, but most of the people live in cities and towns. Farmers grow and sell cotton, tobacco, and rice. They raise chickens, cattle, and horses.

Cities in the Upper South are important places for business. Memphis is a busy transportation center and distribution hub. Big highways, train lines, and the Mississippi River pass through Memphis. Many people in Memphis work to distribute goods throughout the world. The health care and tourism industries are also very important.

Tourists enjoy outdoor activities. They can hunt for diamonds in an Arkansas diamond mine. Music lovers go to Nashville to hear country music. History lovers visit the homes of George Washington and Thomas Jefferson. They can also visit Colonial Williamsburg.

Working in the Upper South

Many companies have moved to the Upper South. They like the region because of its mild climate and educated workers. Many people work in transportation, farming, and tourism. Manufacturing, especially of textiles, is an important industry in the Upper South. More than half the furniture sold in the United States is made in High Point, North Carolina. Mining makes West Virginia a leading producer of coal.

The biggest research center in the United States, Research Triangle Park, is in North Carolina. About 45,000 people work there. They explore new ideas in medicine, computers, and communications. New forms of communication use technology to send messages quickly over long distances. They include cell phones, e-mail, and the Internet.

Before You Read

Find and underline each vocabulary word.

transportation *noun*, the business of carrying people or goods from one place to another

hub *noun*, a major center of activity

research *verb*, to study something carefully to learn more about it

communication *noun*, the exchange of information

After You Read

REVIEW What makes Memphis an important business center? Draw a box around the paragraph that tells why Memphis is special.

REVIEW Describe two of the major industries of the Upper South. Circle words that name industries.

Summary: What's Special About the Lower South

Where People Live

There are eight states in the Lower South: Texas, Oklahoma, Louisiana, Mississippi, Alabama, Florida, Georgia, and South Carolina. The climate of the Lower South is mostly warm and damp. Texas and Oklahoma are mostly dry. Many ethnic groups live in the region. Many Cuban Americans, Puerto Ricans, Seminole Indians, and African Americans live in Florida. Cajuns and Creoles live in Louisiana.

Houston is the largest city in the South. Oil was found near Houston in 1901. The Houston Ship Channel was built in 1914. It connected Houston to Galveston Bay on the Gulf of Mexico. Today, Houston is one of the three biggest U.S. ports. The world's biggest medical center is also in Houston. The NASA/Johnson Space Center is nearby. Many people in Houston live in planned communities. There are also rural areas in the Lower South. The only state in the Lower South without a coastline is Oklahoma. Many people catch and sell seafood, especially shrimp. In Mississippi, people raise and sell catfish. Texas has big cattle ranches. People in Florida grow oranges and other fruits.

Work and Recreation

The mild climate makes tourism an important industry in the Lower South. Tourists enjoy hiking, rafting, and fishing. They go to Florida's theme parks. The Mississippi Delta region is the birthplace of a type of music called the blues. New Orleans is the home of jazz. Cajun and zydeco music are popular in Louisiana. Thousands of people work in the four space research centers located in the Lower South. Scientists in Louisiana research pollution.

Before You Read

Find and underline each vocabulary word.

ethnic group *noun*, people who share the same culture, including language, music, food, and art

planned community *noun*, a place to live that is mapped out ahead of time

pollution *noun*, anything that makes the land, water, or air impure or dirty

After You Read

REVIEW How did natural resources affect the growth of Houston? Underline the sentence that tells you what happened in 1901.

REVIEW What are two kinds of work people do in the Lower South? Highlight sentences that tell about work people do.

Resources for Reaching All Learners

16

Use with *States and Regions*, pp. 170–173

Summary: Land and Climate

Land and Water of the Midwest

The Midwest lies in the middle of the country. Canada lies to the north. The Midwest is mostly flat, with some hilly areas. The Great Lakes are in the eastern part of this region. This area has deep forests. In the north, pine forests can survive the cold winters. The Great Plains lie to the west of the Great Lakes. In these states, the climate is drier. Prairie grasses cover much of the land. Farmers turned prairies into farmland. They grow corn and wheat.

The five Great Lakes are the world's largest body of fresh water. Glaciers created these five lakes. Rivers and canals connect them to the Atlantic Ocean and the Gulf of Mexico. Ships can reach the lakes through these waterways.

The Mississippi River is another great waterway. With its tributaries, the Missouri and Ohio rivers, it is part of the largest river system in the country. Dams and levees help stop flooding. Locks on waterways help ships pass waterfalls. Before railroads, travel on waterways was faster and less expensive than traveling on land.

Climate, Plants, Animals

The Midwest can have severe weather. It has no ocean nearby to warm the land in winter and cool it in the summer. The Great Lakes are not as big as an ocean, but they affect the climate. They add moisture to the air.

Winters are cold, and there are big snowstorms called blizzards. People wear layers of clothes and use covered walkways. They go skiing, skating, and ice fishing. In the summer, there are tornadoes with strong, whirling winds.

Plants and animals also adapt to the climate. Prairie grass has deep roots to find water. Some birds migrate to warmer places in the winter. Prairie dogs live underground. Buffalo once lived on the Great Plains. They had thick fur. Hunters killed most of them for their skins. Then people started protecting buffalo. Now there are about 150,000 buffalo in the United States.

Before You Read

Find and underline each vocabulary word.

prairie *noun*, dry, mostly flat grassland with few trees

tributary *noun*, a river or stream that flows into another river

levee *noun*, a high river bank that stops the river from overflowing

lock *noun*, part of a waterway that is closed off by gates

After You Read

REVIEW **What are the major regions and waterways of the Midwest?** Circle the words that name a region or waterway of the Midwest.

REVIEW **How have people and wildlife adapted to the climate of the Midwest?** Underline sentences tell what people, animals and plants do to survive in cold winters and hot summers.

Summary: Resources and Economy

Using Midwestern Resources

The Midwest has many natural resources. Water, rich soil, and minerals helped the region become a major farming and manufacturing center. Water is an important resource. Farmers water crops with it. Rivers and lakes provide transportation.

Large manufacturing cities have grown along waterways. The rich soil and climate support forests that provide lumber and other wood products. The Midwest produces corn, wheat, and soybeans. Farmers also grow hay, fruits, and vegetables. They raise hogs and dairy cows. Some workers make food products, such as jam or cereal. Others build tractors. Miners dig minerals from the ground. Lead is used to make batteries and computers. Iron ore is used to make steel. Steel is used to make cars, boats, planes, and bridges.

The Midwest's Economy

Many manufacturers build factories in the Midwest. The region has many natural resources. It has skilled workers. It has waterways for moving goods. Service industries also have grown in the Midwest. People in the transportation industry provide a service. They move raw materials to factories and finished products to stores. Indianapolis, Chicago, and Kansas City are important transportation hubs. Banking, health services, and communications are also important service industries.

The concepts of supply and demand can help you understand the economy. The supply is how much of a product producers make. The demand is how much of that product consumers will buy at different prices. If there is a big demand for a product and a small supply, the producer may raise the price of the product.

For example, a company makes a new cereal. If many people want to buy it, the price rises. People pay more for it. But if the price is too high, people may stop buying. The demand for the product falls. If demand stays high, the company will make more. As the supply rises, the price drops. The government helps farmers when supply and demand vary by keeping farm prices from dropping too low.

Before You Read

Find and underline each vocabulary word.

supply *noun*, how much of a product producers will make at different prices

demand *noun*, how much of a product consumers will buy at different prices

After You Read

REVIEW **Name two midwestern industries.** Circle two words that tell what the Midwest is a center for.

REVIEW **Why have certain businesses grown in the Midwest?** There are three reasons why businesses grew in the Midwest. Draw a box around the sentences that name the reasons.

18   Use with *States and Regions*, pp. 196–199

Summary: People of the Midwest

The Midwest's First People

American Indians have lived in the Midwest for centuries. Each Indian nation has its own culture. Woodland Indians farmed and built houses with wood frames. Plains Indians followed and hunted the buffalo herds on the Great Plains. Spanish explorers brought the first horses to North America. Soon Plains Indians were using horses to hunt and travel.

Indians traded furs with Europeans for metal tools. Europeans took land to settle. England and France went to war for control of the Ohio Valley. Pontiac, leader of the Ottawa, fought against the English. In 1763 the British defeated the French. The Ottawa were defeated two years later. About 4,700 Ottawa still live in the area.

Early Settlers

The United States took control of the Northwest Territory in 1783. In 1803, Thomas Jefferson bought the Louisiana Territory from France. Jefferson sent Lewis and Clark to explore the region.

Congress passed the Homestead Act of 1862. It gave land to anyone who would settle and stay for five years. Settlers and immigrants from the east came to farm. The government gave land to soldiers. Life was often hard. There were not enough trees to build wooden houses. People built houses of sod. The Indians were pushed from their land. Most were forced to live on reservations.

Midwestern Cities

Midwestern cities grew because of industry and transportation routes. In the late 1800s, many people moved from farms to cities to find factory jobs. Factories used the assembly line to make goods cheaply and quickly.

After World War I, many African Americans moved to the Midwest to get factory work. St. Louis and Minneapolis grew because they were close to natural resources and the Mississippi River. The river provided power for mills. These cities became manufacturing and food processing centers.

Before You Read

Find and underline each vocabulary word.

homestead *noun*, a piece of land given to someone to settle and farm there

reservation *noun*, land set aside by the government for American Indians

assembly line *noun*, a way of manufacturing goods where each worker does one small part of the job

After You Read

REVIEW How did horses change the lives of the Plains Indians long ago? Circle the sentence that tells you the answer.

REVIEW What were two reasons that the United States grew? Highlight the sentences that tell how the United States got more land.

REVIEW Why did midwestern cities grow? Underline the sentence that tells you the answer.

Resources for Reaching All Learners
19   Use with *States and Regions*, pp. 204–209

Summary: What's Special About the Great Lakes States

Where People Live

The Great Lakes states are Ohio, Indiana, Illinois, Michigan, Wisconsin, and Minnesota. Each state borders a Great Lake. The northern states, Michigan, Wisconsin, and Minnesota, have thick forests. The southern Great Lakes states have good farmland. Most people live in cities or in suburbs near cities.

Chicago is the biggest city in the region. It is an important center for business, manufacturing, and transportation because of its location near waterways. As Chicago grew, the city built public transportation. The elevated train carries many people without getting in the way of busy city traffic.

The Great Lakes states also have more than 400,000 farms. In recent years, farmers started using more machines and fewer workers to grow crops. People in rural areas usually earn lower wages, but they also pay less for living than city people.

Tourists visit the Great Lakes states to camp, fish, boat, or swim. Winter activities like snowmobiling and ice fishing are popular. In cities, people like to visit sports arenas and museums.

Leaving Cities

People once moved to cities looking for better jobs and lives than they had in rural areas. Now many people live in the suburbs and travel to cities to work and shop. Some businesses have moved to the suburbs. Some people can work at home using new technology. Cities have problems when people leave. Buildings and homes may be empty, and crime rises. Fast-growing suburbs can also cause environmental problems. Building may not leave enough natural areas for people to enjoy. Air pollution increases because many people drive instead of walking. Cities like Detroit are rebuilding their downtowns to get people to live there again. Cities also work to improve public transportation and protect open space. This may improve life in some cities.

Before You Read

Find and underline each vocabulary word.

elevated train *noun,* a railway that runs above the ground on raised tracks

wages *noun,* the payments for work

After You Read

REVIEW **What is an advantage of the elevated train?** Circle the words that tell why the train works well in Chicago.

REVIEW **How can the growth of suburbs affect the environment?** Underline two sentences that tell why suburbs can cause environmental problems.

Summary: The Plains States

Where People Live

The Plains States are North Dakota, South Dakota, Nebraska, Kansas, Iowa, and Missouri. Iowa and Missouri are in the Central Lowlands, a region with deep fertile soil. The other Plains States are higher, drier, and rockier. They have sandhills and badlands. Wind and water made unusual shapes in the land.

Most major cities formed near rivers. In the past it was easier for people to travel on waterways than across land. Most people in the Plains States live in cities, but most of the land is rural. Rural areas have a low population density. For example, in a city, 5,000 people might live in a square mile. In a rural area, only one person might live in an area twice that size. Small towns have fewer people. They also have fewer services and businesses, such as stores or restaurants. Some rural communities have big fairs where farmers show their best animals. People enjoy horseback riding, fishing, and hunting.

Rural Lands on the Plains

Much of the Plains States was once a huge prairie. Farmers made farmland by plowing most of the prairie that covered the Great Plains. They use the land for growing crops and raising cattle for beef. Water towers and grain elevators may be the only tall buildings between one town and the next. Tourists visit the area to see Mount Rushmore, a huge sculpture of American presidents, and natural wonders such as Chimney Rock in Nebraska.

American Indians followed buffalo herds on the Great Plains for centuries. As the United States grew, the U.S. army fought the Indians and took their land. The United States broke many promises it made with the Indian nations. The U.S. government created reservations. Indians were forced to live on reservations. The Lakota nation, also called the Sioux, has two large reservations in South Dakota.

Before You Read

Find and underline each vocabulary word.

population density *noun,* a measure of how many people live in an area

grain elevator *noun,* a building used to store wheat or other grains

After You Read

REVIEW **Where are most major cities of the Plains States located?** Highlight the sentence that explains why cities formed near rivers.

REVIEW **In what ways do people use the rural areas of the Plains States?** Underline a sentence that tells how farmers use the land. Circle three popular activities people enjoy.

Resources for Reaching All Learners
21
Use with *States and Regions,* pp. 228–231

Summary: Land and Climate

Land and Water of the West

The West is divided into the Southwest, Mountain, and Pacific States. Most western states are east of the Pacific Ocean between Mexico and Canada. Alaska and Hawaii are separated from the other states by land and water. The West has many different landforms and climate regions. There are mountain ranges and valleys, deserts and rain forests, glaciers and volcanoes.

The Rocky Mountains formed as tectonic plates pushed against each other. This caused the earth's crust to fold. The Cascade Mountains formed when melted lava from a volcano bubbled up through openings in the earth's crust. This released geothermal energy. Between the mountain ranges there are valleys, basins, and flat, raised areas called plateaus. Glaciers carved valleys such as Yosemite Valley. Rivers wore away the rock and made deep canyons, like the Grand Canyon.

Water, Climate, and Wildlife

Many rivers flow west from the Rockies. The water is used for irrigation. Most people live on the coast because the land is so dry. Dams are used to produce hydroelectric power.

Temperatures in the West are affected by the Pacific Ocean, elevation, and latitude. Cool, moist air flows east from the Pacific Ocean. This gives the northern coast mild temperatures and more rain than the south. As moist air goes over the mountains, it drops rain and snow on the western side. This air is dry as it goes down the eastern side. This makes the climate arid. Places at high elevations are colder. Alaska is in the northern latitudes, so it has short summers and long winters.

Plants and animals depend on climate. Tropical plants grow in Hawaii. Cactuses grow in arid areas. Sequoias and redwoods grow in wet coastal areas. Bristlecone pines live in the mountains. Elk, bighorn sheep, and cougars live there too. Lizards, scorpions, and snakes live in the hot dry Southwest. In Alaska there are moose, bears, and condors.

Before You Read

Find and underline each vocabulary word.

geothermal *adjective*, heat from beneath the Earth's crust

irrigation *noun*, a way of supplying land with water

hydroelectric power *noun*, electricity produced from flowing water

arid *adjective*, very dry

After You Read

REVIEW **What are three major landforms found in the West?** Circle words that name landforms. Draw a box around the names of specific landforms.

REVIEW **What factors influence temperature in the West?** Underline the sentence that tells you the answer.

Summary: Resources and Economy

Using Resources

People in the West use their natural resources to make goods and sell services. Soil and climate are important resources. Farmers grow fruit and vegetables to sell. Many people have jobs processing and shipping food. Trees are also a key resource. People cut trees down and make them into lumber and paper at mills. People catch fish in the ocean.

The West's climate helps many businesses. People make movies and tourists come for vacations. Aircraft companies build airplanes. People mine natural mineral resources, such as copper, gold, uranium, and coal. Other people make products from the minerals. The U.S. government owns a lot of land in the West. Some of it is in national parks, such as Glacier, Yellowstone, and Grand Canyon.

The West's Economy

Many businesses in the West do research or provide services. Many companies in the West make computer products, software, or aircraft. Technology is important to the economy, especially in the Southwest and Pacific States. Many businesses have a specialization. For example, a company might make just one part of a computer, not the whole computer. The company can improve how that part works and also learn to make it at a lower cost.

Some people are skilled workers. They have special training or education. For example, many people in the computer industry have advanced training. They research and invent computer products. For some jobs, workers need no special training. Businesses can hire unskilled workers. Skilled workers usually make more money than unskilled workers.

Many people in Hawaii and Alaska work for the government. In all regions of the West many people work in service jobs, like health care or construction.

Before You Read

Find and underline each vocabulary word.

national park *noun,* an area of land set aside by the federal government

specialization *noun,* when a business makes only a few goods or provides just one service

skilled worker *noun,* someone who has special training or education to do a job

unskilled worker *noun,* someone who does not need special training or education to do a job

After You Read

REVIEW What are two ways that people use resources in the West? Underline two sentences that tell what resources people in the West grow or use.

REVIEW Which parts of the West have the most technology companies? Draw a box around the sentence that tells where technology is important to the economy.

Summary: The People of the West

Early Peoples of the West

Many scientists think people first came to the West over 15,000 years ago. The Aleut and Inuit lived in the North. The Hopi and Navajo lived in the Southwest. They learned to use the resources where they lived. Those near the sea fished. Others hunted and farmed.

About 700 years ago, people we now call the Pueblo people lived near the Rio Grande. They irrigated land to grow crops. They gathered wild plants and hunted animals. They made baskets and pottery and traded them for salt, food, and animal hides. On the northwest coast, the Tlingit people gathered wild plants, hunted, and fished. They traded seal oil for furs and made blankets that showed stories. Pueblo, Tlingit, and other American Indian groups still live in the West.

Spanish Settlements

The Spanish conquered Mexico in 1519 and called it New Spain. Then they went north to look for gold. The Spanish took the Indians' land. The Spanish wanted Indians to give up their culture and become Christians, so they started missions.

In 1821, Mexico won independence from Spain. Texas split off from Mexico in 1836 and joined the United States in 1845. Mexico and the United States went to war the following year. The United States won. Mexico had to give the Southwest to the United States. Spanish and Mexican influence is still strong there. Many people speak Spanish. Many foods and festivals in the region come from Spain or Mexico.

More People Go West

Gold was found in California in 1848. Many people moved west in wagon trains hoping to get rich or buy cheap land. They took American Indian land. American Indians were forced to move to separate places called reservations. After Chinese immigrants helped build the transcontinental railroad in 1869, the West grew fast. In 1959, Hawaii and Alaska were the last two states to join the Union. Now there are 50 states.

Before You Read

Find and underline each vocabulary word.

mission *noun,* a settlement for teaching religion to local people

wagon train *noun,* a line of wagons that carried settlers and their belongings

transcontinental railroad *noun,* train system that linked the East and the West

After You Read

REVIEW What did different groups who settled the West have in common? Underline a sentence that tells what the Aleut, Inuit, Hopi, and Navajo learned to use in the West.

REVIEW Why did the Spanish build missions in New Spain? Draw a box around the words that tell the answer.

REVIEW How did the transcontinental railroad affect population in the West? Circle the words that tell what happened to the population after the transcontinental railroad was built.

Use with *States and Regions,* pp. 262–267

Summary: The Southwest

Where People Live

The four Southwest states are Utah, Nevada, New Mexico, and Arizona. The climate is dry. They have mountains, plateaus, deserts, and other landforms.

Big cities grew in the deserts. Phoenix is the largest city in the Southwest. The first people to live there were the Hohokam. They built irrigation canals to water their crops. Later, European settlers found the canals and rebuilt the settlement. They built dams on rivers to provide water. Today, Phoenix has a steady supply of water. Over one million people live there. Buildings in Phoenix are made in Spanish, Mexican, and American Indian styles.

Thousands of American Indians live in the Southwest in cities and on pueblos. The Navajo Indian reservation is the largest in the nation. It covers 16 million acres in Arizona, New Mexico, and Utah. The Pueblo, Hopi, Zuni, Acoma, and Laguna Indians live in pueblos near the Rio Grande. Some of the oldest ranches in North America are in the Southwest. People raise sheep, cattle, and horses on these ranches.

The Southwest Today

Millions of tourists come to the Southwest each year. They want to see the high mountains, wild rivers, and beautiful canyons. Weathering and erosion carved the Grand Canyon and many natural arches in Utah. There are ghost towns and national parks to visit. People ride bicycles and hike. They paddle the rivers and swim in lakes. They can enjoy Mexican food, Indian festivals, and rodeos. People in the Southwest speak English, Spanish, and Indian languages.

Water is scarce in this region. Reservoirs are made to store water. People practice water conservation. Plants that don't need extra watering are used in parks and public places. Farmers conserve water by using drip irrigation. Drip irrigation does not flood the fields with water. It allows water to slowly soak into the soil.

Before You Read

Find and underline each vocabulary word.

weathering *noun*, the breakdown of rock caused by wind, water, and weather

conservation *noun*, using something carefully and not wasting it

After You Read

REVIEW **Describe how the Spanish, Mexicans, and American Indians have influenced life in the Southwest.** Who were the first people to live in Phoenix? How did they get water? Which American Indian groups live in the Southwest today? Buildings in Phoenix are made in different styles. What are they? Circle the words and sentences that tell you the answers.

REVIEW **How do people conserve water?** What kinds of plants are used in parks and public places? How do farmers conserve water? Underline the sentences that tell you the answers.

Summary: What's Special About the Mountain States

Cities and Rural Areas

The Rocky Mountains run through Colorado, Idaho, Montana, and Wyoming. These states are called the Mountain States. There are also hills, plateaus, plains, and valleys. The Sioux, Cheyenne, Arapaho, Apache, Ute, and Crow Indians were the first people to live in the region.

Denver is the capital of Colorado. It is on a mile-high plain east of the Rockies. The mountains block moisture coming from the west. This keeps the climate dry.

Most people in the Mountain States live in the cities. The cities are centers for entertainment, education, and health care. Some people live in rural areas. Here, the land is rugged. The winters are long and cold. People raise cattle and sheep. There are usually only a few doctors, dentists, schools, and other services in these areas. People living in rural areas travel to cities to get supplies and services.

Recreation and Tourism

Many people work in mining, farming, and forestry industries in the Mountain States. Tourism is also an important industry. The high elevation of the Mountain States creates a perfect place for winter sports. Tourists come to ski in the winter. They camp, hike, fish, and ride horses in the summer. Tourists spend money and buy services, such as hotels and meals. Tourism creates jobs.

There are many national parks in the region, including Yellowstone and Glacier. National parks protect wilderness areas and historical places. Yellowstone is the nation's oldest national park. It is a complete ecosystem with many different habitats. Animals like the buffalo were almost extinct. Now they are protected in the park. Yellowstone is also famous for its geysers. The heat inside the earth causes geysers to shoot out hot water. Visitors can also see hot springs and bubbling mud pots.

Before You Read

Find and underline each vocabulary word.

ecosystem *noun*, an environment and all its living things, working together as a unit

habitat *noun*, the natural home of a plant or animal

extinct *adjective*, no longer existing

After You Read

REVIEW **Name two things the four Mountain States have in common.** Circle the landforms that the Mountain States share. Highlight a sentence that tells where most people live.

REVIEW **What attracts visitors to the Mountain States?** What do tourists do in the summer and the winter? Which national parks can they visit? Underline the sentences that tell the answers.

Summary: What's Special About the Pacific States

Cities of the Pacific States

The Pacific States are Alaska, California, Oregon, Washington, and Hawaii. Four states are on the coast of the Pacific Ocean. The fifth, Hawaii, is a group of islands in the middle of the Pacific. The ocean affects the climate of all these states.

Seattle is Washington State's biggest city. It is a center for business and industry. Many people there work in technology industries. Other big cities in the Pacific States are port cities, such as Portland, Oregon, Los Angeles, California, and Honolulu, Hawaii. Ships from these ports carry goods all over the world. San Francisco, California, is an international banking center. Los Angeles is home to the movie and television industry.

Agricultural Activities

The different climates of the Pacific States let farmers grow many crops. It is cool and wet in the northwest coastal regions. Farmers grow peas, pears, broccoli, apples, and strawberries.

East of the Cascade Mountains, farmers grow wheat and sugar beets. In southern California, where the growing season is very long, farmers can grow citrus fruits, almonds, kiwi, and figs. In tropical Hawaii, they grow 650,000 tons of pineapple a year.

Harvesting, or picking the crops, is seasonal work. Each crop is picked at a certain time of year. Farmers need migrant workers to do this work. Many migrant workers live in bad conditions and are paid very little.

The cities on the coast support farming in rural areas. Cities have factories where farm crops are turned into food products. Workers in factories can fruits and vegetables, make juices, and bake goods.

Tourists in the Pacific States enjoy skiing, surfing, and visiting national parks. They can see Arctic wilderness in Alaska, active volcanoes in Hawaii, and glaciers and a rainforest in Washington State.

Before You Read

Find and underline each vocabulary word.

seasonal *adjective,* happening at certain times of the year

migrant worker *noun,* a worker who moves from place to place to find seasonal work

After You Read

REVIEW What is the importance of the seaports on the Pacific coast? Underline the sentence that tells what happens at port cities.

REVIEW What industries support farming in the Pacific States? Draw a box around two sentences that tell how farm crops are turned into food products.

Summary: United States Government

Government by the People

One role of our government is to protect our rights. The United States government is "by the people." This means that the people create the government and decide who will lead them. Our government is "of the people." This means that each citizen has a say in the government. Our government is "for the people" because it is for the good of everyone.

The United States is a democracy. The people decide who will lead and what the government will do. But there are too many people to vote on every decision. So people choose representatives, who vote for them in the government. Representatives make decisions and represent the people. Citizens vote for representatives in an election.

Before 1776, the states were colonies ruled by Great Britain. People in the colonies wanted to be free from British rule. They wrote the Declaration of Independence to explain why they wanted to break ties with Britain.

The Constitution

The leaders of the United States wrote the Constitution in 1787. The Bill of Rights is part of the Constitution. It protects our rights and freedoms. It makes sure all citizens have freedom, equality, and justice. The Bill of Rights also limits the powers of the government.

The Constitution set up three branches of government. This helps make sure that one branch does not get too powerful. The legislative branch makes laws. Citizens elect representatives to Congress. Congress has two parts, the House of Representatives and the Senate. The executive branch carries out the laws. The President is head of the executive branch. The judicial branch decides questions about the laws. This branch includes the courts. The Supreme Court is the highest court in the United States. It has the final say on laws. The Supreme Court decides what laws mean and if they are allowed by the Constitution.

Before You Read

Find and underline each vocabulary word.

citizen *noun*, a person born in a country or who promises to be loyal to the country

democracy *noun*, a system in which the people hold the power of government

representative *noun*, a person who acts for a group of people

election *noun*, the way voters choose people to serve in government

constitution *noun*, a plan for setting up and running a government

After You Read

REVIEW **What is the job of representatives in our democratic system?** Underline the words that tell what representatives do for the people who elect them.

REVIEW **Why are there three branches of government?** The Constitution set up three branches of government. Why? Draw a box around the sentence that tells the answer.

Use with *States and Regions*, pp. 308–311

Summary: Many Regions, One Nation

Linking Regions

Americans share the same government. We have the same values of liberty, equality, and justice. Our nation is connected by railroads, canals, and airports. We are linked by phones, airplanes, and the Internet.

Each connection between states leads to interdependence. For example, farmers in Maryland can sell their crops to families in New Jersey. People in New Jersey can buy food from farmers in Maryland. The farmers and families both depend on each other. These kinds of links are found across the country. They help to bring us together.

The U.S. government works hard to create these links. The U.S. Postal Service connects people and businesses across the country. It helps people communicate and move goods. The government also helped to build a transportation system across the country. The Interstate Highway system helps transport people and goods around the country.

Good transportation and communication help bring prosperity to Americans. The government runs air-traffic control so that airplanes can travel safely. It sets basic rules for television and radio communications. The government and businesses try to make trade grow. The banking system makes trade easier because everyone knows how to pay for goods and services.

Our Common Culture

Americans come from many different places, but we have a shared heritage. This includes language, food, music, holidays, and beliefs. The cultures of all people who live in the United States are part of our heritage. People in every state celebrate Independence Day with fireworks and Memorial Day with parades. People from all regions help when there is need. After the attacks on September 11, 2001, volunteers came to New York City from all over the country to help.

Before You Read

Find and underline each vocabulary word.

interdependence *noun,* a relationship in which people depend on each other

prosperity *noun,* wealth and success

heritage *noun,* traditions that people have honored for many years

volunteer *noun,* someone who agrees to provide a service without pay

After You Read

REVIEW In what ways does the United States Postal Service link different parts of the country? Underline the sentence that tells what the U.S. postal service does.

REVIEW In what ways do we show our shared culture? Draw a box around the sentence that describes how people celebrate holidays all over the country.

Use with *States and Regions,* pp. 314–317

Summary: North American Neighbors

Our Northern Neighbor: Canada

The United States is part of North America. Canada is also in North America. It is north of the United States. Canada is the second largest country in the world in land area. But the United States has nine times more people. The United States trades with Canada more than any other country.

Canada stretches far north into the Arctic Circle, so the climate is cold. Mountain ranges on the coast block warm winds from the Pacific Ocean. Most people live where it is warmer, on the coasts or on the southern border.

The United States and Canada share landforms, such as the Rocky Mountains and the Great Plains. Forestry is a major industry in Canada.

American Indians have lived in Canada for thousands of years. Settlers from France and Britain came in the 1600s. In Quebec, many people speak French. In other parts of Canada people mostly speak English. Canada has ten provinces and three territories.

Mexico and the Caribbean

Mexico is on the southern border of the United States. It is large and has many regions. The capital, Mexico City, is on the Mexican Plateau. It is one of the world's biggest cities. Mountain ranges go down both coasts. It can be cold in the mountains, but the climate of Mexico is mostly tropical, warm, and dry. The United States trades a lot with Mexico and the Caribbean islands.

The Caribbean islands are southeast of the United States. American Indians lived in the Caribbean and Mexico for thousands of years. In the 1400s, European countries took land for colonies. Spain conquered the Aztec people of Mexico. Spain and other European nations also colonized Caribbean islands. Europeans brought enslaved Africans to the area. Today, most Mexicans speak Spanish and have Spanish or Indian backgrounds. Many people in the Caribbean have African backgrounds.

Before You Read

Find and underline the vocabulary word.

province *noun,* a unit of government into which a nation is divided

After You Read

REVIEW How do Canada's area and population compare to those of the United States? Underline the sentences that tell about Canada's size and how many people live there compared to the United States.

REVIEW In what ways is the history of Mexico and the Caribbean like the history of the United States? Circle the sentence that tells who lived in Mexico and the Caribbean before Europeans arrived. Draw a box around the sentence that tells what the Europeans did when they arrived. Then underline the sentence that tells how Africans came to these places.

Summary: Central and South America

Central America

Central America has seven countries. They are all part of North America. Central America is long and narrow. The isthmus of Panama, at the southern end, is only about 50 miles wide. The United States took the land in 1903 and built a canal so ships could go from the Atlantic to the Pacific oceans. The Panama Canal opened in 1914.

Mountains run down the middle of Central America. Central America is tropical. There are rain forests with many kinds of plants and animals. American Indians, such as the Maya, have lived there for thousands of years. Then European countries, such as Spain and England, took land for colonies. Today there are people of Spanish, American Indian, and mixed background.

Agriculture is an important industry in Central America. Major crops are bananas, sugar, and coffee. Many people are poor and only grow enough to live.

South America

South America has twelve countries. It is just south of Central America. A major landform is the Andes Mountains. There are high peaks and some volcanoes. The Amazon River flows through the world's largest rain forest. Much of South America is tropical, with a wet, hot climate. But in the mountains, temperatures can be cold. The southern part of the continent almost reaches the frozen continent of Antarctica.

American Indians have lived in South America for thousands of years. In the 1500s, Spain and Portugal took over most of South America. They forced the Indians to work for them and also brought enslaved Africans. Later, immigrants from Europe and Asia came to live in South America.

South America is rich in minerals, oil, and metals. Industry is growing, but most people farm. Other resources are the plants in the forest. South Americans are working hard to protect the rain forest. Industry is growing, but most people live by farming.

Before You Read

Find and underline each vocabulary word.

isthmus *noun,* a narrow strip of land that connects two larger land areas

rain forest *noun,* dense forest that gets large amounts of rainfall every year

After You Read

REVIEW **What made Panama a good place to build a canal?** Draw a box around the sentence that tells how wide Panama is.

REVIEW **Name two major physical features of the South American continent.** Circle the names of a major landform and a river in South America.

Summary: World Regions

Regions of the World

People divide the world into different kinds of regions. A region has some shared features, such as landforms, history, culture, or crops. Hemispheres are regions that include half of the earth. The United States is in the Northern and Western Hemispheres. Continents are another kind of region. The United States is part of the North American continent.

Landform regions can be identified by common landforms. They are based on the shape of the land. Mountain regions may be rugged with steep slopes. Plains regions may have broad, flat land. Continents have many landform regions. Climate regions, such as Arctic zones and tropical zones, are another way people divide the world. Regions can be defined by the amount of rainfall they get or by vegetation. Regions can also be defined by human features, such as a shared economic system, language, or religion.

Regions and People

The features of a region affect the lives of its people. For example, the warm, wet climate of Southeast Asia is good for growing rice. Rice is the most important food there and in most of Asia. Rice plays a role in the religions of Asia. In Bali people think of rice as a great gift and have religious ceremonies to show their respect. People who live in arctic regions cannot farm because it is too cold. Fishing and hunting are central to their lives. Resources of a region also affect how people live. In forested regions, people build their houses of wood. In warmer regions, people build houses of cement to stay cool. There can be differences within regions too. In India there are people who speak different dialects and have different religious beliefs. Different kinds of regions can overlap. A mountain region can include two different language regions. Learning about regions helps us understand the world and the people in it.

Before You Read

Find and underline each vocabulary word.

vegetation *noun*, the kinds of plants that grow in a region

dialect *noun*, a regional form of a language

After You Read

REVIEW **What are two kinds of regions?** Highlight words that name kinds of regions.

REVIEW **How can the features of a region affect the people who live there?** Underline sentences that tell how climate or natural resources affect how people in Southeast Asia live. Underline sentences that tell about houses people build.

Resources for Reaching All Learners

32

Use with *States and Regions*, pp. 340–343

Summary: Partners Around the World

United States Allies

The United States has many allies. The United States forms alliances, or agreements, with other countries. Allies help defend each other. The United States also has alliances for trading and sharing scientific research. Alliances are formed by making treaties. The North Atlantic Treaty Organization, NATO, was formed in 1949 between the United States and our European allies. NATO countries agree to defend each other from attack. The North American Free Trade Agreement, or NAFTA, is a trade alliance. It lets Mexico, Canada, and the United States buy and sell goods to each other without paying fees or taxes. The United States also has allies on other continents. Many of our allies believe in a free enterprise system. The United States also trades with countries that do not believe in free enterprise.

Trading Partners

Trade alliances help connect countries through communication and transportation links. These links let goods, services, and information move freely. When businesses sell their goods to people in other countries they can sell more, so trade grows. International trade is the buying and selling of goods between countries. It is an important part of our economy. U.S. businesses sell goods and services worth hundreds of billions of dollars to other countries every year. U.S. consumers also buy hundreds of billions of dollars in imports or goods that come from other countries. Some imported goods cost less than goods made in the United States. People buy cars, clothing, and television sets from other countries. Many people worry that free trade hurts American workers. They think we need laws to protect jobs and the environment. Some countries pass laws to add extra cost to imports. The United States has rules to protect some industries, but also supports free trade. Canada and Mexico are our biggest trading partners. We also trade with China, Japan, South Korea, and nations in Europe. Many European nations formed the European Union trade alliance.

Before You Read

Find and underline each vocabulary word.

ally *noun*, a country or group that joins with another country or group for a common purpose

alliance *noun*, an agreement between allies to seek a common goal

treaty *noun*, an official document that defines an agreement between nations

free enterprise *noun*, a system that lets people control their businesses and decide what goods to buy

import *noun*, a product brought in from another country

After You Read

REVIEW Why does the United States form alliances? Highlight the sentences that tell you the answer.

REVIEW Why is international trade important to the United States? Underline the sentence that tells why selling to people in other countries makes trade grow.

Resources for Reaching All Learners
33 Use with *States and Regions*, pp. 348–351

Summary: Working Together

Nations Work Together

The United States works with other countries for common goals. After World War II, the United States helped create the United Nations, or UN, to build peace and friendship around the world.

More than 190 countries belong to the UN. Members work together to solve problems. Members wrote the Universal Declaration of Human Rights to protect everyone's basic rights. The World Bank, part of the UN, helps countries build their economies. The World Health Organization works to improve health worldwide. The United States and many other countries have agreed to some basic rules. They are called international law. For example, many countries have agreed on what can and cannot be done in war. Treaties are another example of international law. The UN helps organize trials if crimes were committed in a war.

People Work Together

Nongovernmental organizations (NGOs), such as the International Red Cross or Doctors Without Borders, cross borders between countries to help people. There are thousands of NGOs in the world. They are not part of any country's government. Many work with the UN. They help the poor and sick, give medical care, teach about farming or business, support democracy, and protect human rights. NGOs help when disasters like earthquakes or wars happen.

It is easier for people around the world to communicate now using wireless phones and the Internet. The Internet lets people share information all over the world. People use email and websites to learn new information. Some countries try to control the information their citizens get. New technologies can connect people. This might help bring freedom and change to many.

Before You Read

Find and underline each vocabulary word.

international law *noun*, a set of basic rules to which the United States and many other countries have agreed

nongovernmental organization *noun*, a group that is not part of a national government

After You Read

REVIEW **When was the United Nations formed, and for what purposes?** Underline the sentence that tells when and why the United Nations was formed.

REVIEW **What are some goals of NGOs?** Underline words that tell what NGOs do.

Challenge Activities

Where Are You?

You have learned about two ways geographers identify exact locations. They tell where a place is in relation to other places, and they use lines of latitude and longitude. Where are you? What hemisphere are you in? What continent are you on? What kind of land do you live on? What bodies of water are nearby? Use a map or globe to locate your community. What is the closest line of latitude? What is the closest line of longitude? Use two ways to show your classmates where you live.

Name That Resource

You have learned about the many natural resources in the United States and some of the ways people use them. Look around your classroom. What resources were used to make the things you see? Is there anything made of wood? of metal? of plastic?

Write the natural resources on sticky notes. Label about a dozen items. For example, put "forest trees" on a wooden table or bookcase. Take your classmates on a walk around the room. Point out each item and explain how you know it was made from that resource.

What's Burning?

You have read that we use fossil fuels to make energy. We use this energy to light and heat our houses. Write a letter to the local power company. Find out where the electricity at your school or home comes from. Is there a power plant nearby? Which fuel is used to make the electricity?

Draw a flow chart to show how the energy gets from its original source, to the power company, and then to your home. Share your chart, letter, and the answer you receive with your classmates.

Resources for Reaching All Learners

35

Use with *States and Regions*

Challenge Activities

What's My Region?

Some regions are defined by natural features, and others by human features. Work with friends to make a set of region cards. On one side, write a category that could be used to define a region, such as "mountains," or "urban." Think of as many categories as you can. Then mix up the cards and deal them with the writing side down. Each player picks a card and looks at it without showing the others. Then that player names places that fit the category. For example, if you turned over the card that said "urban," you could name big cities. The other players have to guess what category you are naming. Use a globe or atlas as a reference.

Keep a Weather Log

How's the weather where you are? Is the temperature high or low? Is it raining? Is the sky clear or cloudy? Keep a weather log for a few weeks. Check the weather every morning and afternoon at the same time. Write the temperature, precipitation, wind conditions, and the date and time of each entry. If possible, put a thermometer outside so you can check the temperature. Use your log to make some general statements about the weather where you live.

If I Lived in . . .

You have learned about the six climate regions. Choose a place that has a different climate from where you live. Use the library or Internet to find out more about that region. How does the climate there affect how people dress, the kinds of houses they live in, the work they do, and the things they do for fun? What foods do they eat? What plants and animals live there? Use props and costumes to present your information to your classmates. Tell them that you live in [your chosen place]. Show them where it is on a map or globe. Tell them what the climate is like and how its location affects the climate. Then tell them about what your life might be like if you lived in that place.

Challenge Activities

Eastward, Ho!

Research a state in the East. Use books in the library or the Internet to find out about its climate and its natural resources. Does it have mountains, plains, or beaches? Are there any bodies of water or rivers? What kinds of trees and animals live there? What kind of houses have the people built? Make a book of what you find. Draw a picture or cut out pictures from magazines to show each subject. Share your book with your class and be ready to answer questions.

Start Your Own Business

You have read about entrepreneurs who start their own businesses. Think of a business that you could start. What goods or services would you provide? What natural resources would you use? What human resources and capital resources would you need? How much money would you need to start your business? Make a plan for your own business. Make a budget to show how much money you would need to spend and how much profit you think you could make. Share your idea with your classmates.

Trading Post

You have read about how American Indians traded goods with European settlers. Europeans traded pots, tools, cloth, and beads for furs from the Indians. Find out more. What kinds of tools and cloth did the Indians use before they traded for these goods? What kind of furs did the Indians trade? Write a report about how Indians and Europeans traded and share it with your class. Be ready to answer questions.

Challenge Activities

Plan a Trip

You learned about two regions of the East: New England and the Mid-Atlantic. Use books, magazines, and the Internet to learn more about a city or area that you would like to visit. Plan a trip to see the sights. Make a plan that includes a timetable and estimated costs. How could you get there? How long would it take? How much would it cost? Where would you stay? How much will that cost? Where will you eat? What specific places do you want to see? What activities do you want to do? Include illustrations with your plan. Present your plan to your classmates and answer questions.

Make a Skyscraper

You read about the Empire State Building. Find out more about the history of skyscrapers using encyclopedias, books, or the Internet. Did you know that people didn't build skyscrapers until elevators were invented?

Now try to make a model skyscraper using drinking straws and paper clips. Experiment to find the best way to make your tower strong. Can you build a skyscraper that is taller than you? Can you build one that can hold up a book? Record your building experiences in a journal. Show your skyscraper to your classmates and tell them how you made it, what difficulties you faced, and how you solved them.

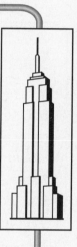

Know Your Public Servants

Who works in your state government? Look for information about the governor, a state senator or representative, or a state judge. Find out more about one of these jobs and the person that does it. What branch of government do they work in? Were they elected or appointed? Write a letter to that person and ask them to tell you about their job. Ask them what challenges they face and what they like about their work. Show your letter and any response to your classmates and tell them about the public servant you investigated.

Challenge Activities

Exploring the Wetlands

The South has a long coastline. Much of this land is
called wetlands. This means that the water is very close
to the surface of the soil. In recent years, laws have been
passed to protect the wetlands. Choose one of the
coastal areas in the South and find out more about the
wetlands there. What animals live there? What plants?
Make a poster using the information you find. Use it to
introduce your classmates to the wetlands.

Storm Tracker

You have read about the storms that affect both the coastal areas and interior
of the South. Look for information about tornados and hurricanes in books,
magazines, and the Internet. Then draw a triptych that shows the story of one
of these storms. Label each frame. The first frame should show how the storm
begins. The second frame should show the storm hitting. The third frame should
show what is left behind after the storm passes. Share your story with your
classmates. Tell them what the storm looks like, how it sounds, what damage
it does, and how it feels after it passes.

What's It Take to Make a T-shirt?

Imagine that you want to sell cotton T-shirts. You start by buying cloth. Is cloth a
raw material, or was it manufactured from something else? Trace the materials
back to the raw materials used. Where did they come from? What processes are
used to change the natural resource into the final product? What kinds of work
do people who make the product do? Create a flow chart that shows the stages
in making a cotton T-shirt. Present your chart to the class and answer questions.

Challenge Activities

Plan a Trip

Choose three places that you would like to visit in the South. Use books, magazines, and Internet sites to learn more about these areas and what you could do there.

Once you have your information, make postcards from your "trip." On the front of an index card, draw a picture of a place. On the back of the card, write about your travels to a classmate. Write about what you did there and what you saw. When you finish, read your postcards to the class.

Follow the Mississippi

The Mississippi River has been important in the history and development of the country. The river passes through several states in the Upper and Lower South. Choose one stretch of the river to focus on. Look for information about this part of the river in books and the Internet.

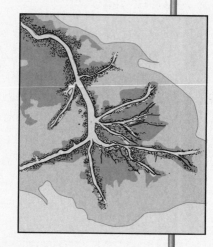

Draw a map that shows the towns and cities along your part of the river. Prepare a presentation for your classmates. Using your map, show your classmates where you are standing and what you can see. Use descriptive language. Include the sights, sounds, and smells of the area.

Space Exploration

The South is home to important centers of space exploration. Find out more about the National Aeronautics and Space Administration (NASA). All of the space centers have websites that tell about their work. Make a poster about the space center and use it to talk with your classmates about space exploration.

Use with *States and Regions*

Challenge Activities

Explore a Great Lake

Together, the five Great Lakes are the largest body of fresh water in the world. Find out more about one of the Great Lakes. How big is it? Is it entirely in the United States? What fish live in it? What big cities are on its shores? How does the lake affect the lives of people who live near it? What kinds of recreation do people enjoy on the lake? Make a poster about the Great Lake you chose. Share it with your classmates.

Trading Post

Europeans traded metal tools for furs and other goods from the American Indians. Look for more information about goods that were traded. Find out how American Indians made their tools and goods before the Europeans came. How did the new tools and goods change the lives of the American Indians?

Draw pictures of different kinds of goods that the American Indians and Europeans exchanged. Cut them out. Write the word for each item on the back of the picture. Set up a trading post with some classmates. Pretend you are American Indians or Europeans and act out trading.

Life on the Prairies

Settlers came to build farms on the prairies after the Homestead Act. Find out more about their lives from books, magazines, and the Internet. What was a sod house like? What kinds of crops did they grow? What challenges did they face?

Make a model of a sod house. Imagine that you lived in one during the 1870s. Invite classmates to see your house and tell them what it was like to live there. Talk about the kinds of tools you had and the crops you grew.

Challenge Activities

Explore Population Density

Build a model that shows population density. You could use information from your school. For example, count the number of students and teachers in each room at a specific time. Remember to include the library, cafeteria, and teachers' lounge. Then make a map that shows the floor plan of your school. If your school has more than one floor, make a plan for each floor. Draw a simple symbol on your floor plan for each person you counted. Do some rooms have a higher population density than others? Share your model with your class.

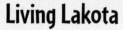

Living Lakota

After the U.S. government took their land, many American Indians lived on reservations. The Great Plains states include two big reservations, Cheyenne River and Pine Ridge. Choose one and find out more about the people who live there now. How many people live on the reservation? What languages do they speak? What kinds of food and recreation do they enjoy? How do they solve problems? Use your library or the Internet to find answers. Then make an imaginary visit to the reservation. Draw pictures and write short descriptions of what you might find there. Share your work with your class and be ready to answer questions.

What Are the Badlands?

Wind and water have carved unusual shapes in the area called the Badlands. The earliest people to come into this area were ancient mammoth hunters more than 11,000 years ago. By the 1750s, Lakota Indians lived in the region. Find out more about Badlands National Park, where people can learn about interesting rocks, fossils, plants, and animals in the area. Make a poster that shows things you might find if you visited. Share what you have learned about the Badlands with your class.

Challenge Activities

Compare and Contrast

Choose two states of the West that are in different regions. Use your library or the Internet to find out more about the land and natural resources of the two states. Make a chart to compare them. Make up questions about each state. For example, what kinds of landforms can you see there? What plants and animals live there? What is the climate like? Are there big cities or is it mostly rural? Tell your classmates about the two states. Tell them which one you would rather visit and why.

Long Journeys

You have read about different journeys people took to go West. The Spanish sailed across the Atlantic Ocean to Mexico. Many people took wagon trains or the railroad. Choose a journey and find out more about it using the library or the Internet. Draw a map to show where the journey began and ended. Then write directions for taking the same journey. For example: "Get on a ship in the harbor of Cadiz. Sail west for 35 days. Land on the coast of Mexico." Show your map to your classmates. Use it to describe your journey. Include how long each part of the journey took. What was the weather like? What things did you see along the way?

Where's the Gold?

The hunt for gold was one reason the Spanish explored and conquered the Americas. When gold was discovered in California in 1848, thousands of people went there. Learn more about panning for gold and using a sluice to separate the rock ore from the gold. Draw a picture of some ways that gold is mined, and then explain it to your classmates. Be ready to answer questions.

Challenge Activities

Amazing Landforms!

You read about the climate and landforms of the West. Have you ever visited a national park? Choose a place you would like to see. You might pick Mauna Loa, the active volcano in Hawaii, or the Grand Canyon in Arizona, or the high peaks of the Rocky Mountains. Use books, magazines, and the Internet to research your location. What kinds of plants and animals live there?

Make a sketch journal of an imaginary trip. Draw pictures to illustrate the things you might see there. Write captions for each picture. Share it with your class.

Urban or Rural?

You read about living in urban areas and rural areas. Do you live in an urban or rural area? Do you live in a suburb? Find out more about your own community. Make a list of questions like the following: How many people live in your community? Do most of them live in apartment buildings or on farms? If you live in a city, where is the nearest farm? What do they grow?

Draw a map of your region. Show where there are cities and where there are farms or ranches. Draw a star to show where you live. Then tell your class about the information that you have gathered.

Hawaii

You read about the tropical climate of Hawaii and the active volcano. Use books, magazines and the Internet to explore Hawaii. How did islands in the middle of the Pacific Ocean become part of the United States? How far are the islands from the west coast of North America? Who lived there before the Europeans came? Who lives there now? Make a poster about Hawaii. Use it to talk with your classmates about what you have learned.

Challenge Activities

Name That Country

Choose one country from each area: North America, Central America, and South America. Write four questions about the landforms and climates, natural resources, history and government, the people and culture, or the work they do. Use the library or Internet to find the answer. Then make a set of cards for each country, with the question and the answer written on one side. On the other side, draw the shape of the country. Ask your classmates to identify the country from the questions and answers. If they guess the wrong country, show them how to compare the shape on a map.

Building the Canal

Before the Panama Canal was built, ships had to sail all the way around the bottom of South America to get to the West coast. Do some research to find out how the canal was built. How does the canal work? Can boats pass in both directions? How long does it take them to go through the canal? How much do ships have to pay to use the canal? Who gets the money? Has the canal changed over time? Make a diorama or poster to show the canal. Show it to your classmates and tell them what you learned about it.

What Are Your Rights?

You have read about how the Constitution was written to start and run the government. The Bill of Rights was added to make sure every person in the United States had the same rights and freedoms. Find out what these rights are. Look for information on the amendments to the Constitution that are included in the Bill of Rights. Make a poster about one of these amendments and rewrite the idea in simple language. Tell your classmates about what you learned.

Resources for Reaching All Learners

45

Use with *States and Regions*

Challenge Activities

Your Home and Other Places

If you could travel anywhere in the world, where would you go? Choose a country that is in a different region. Learn more about it using books, magazines, and the Internet. Now choose two categories, like landforms, climate, or animals that live there. Make a chart to compare where you live to the country you chose. What things do they have in common? How are they different? Share your finished chart with your classmates.

Where Was It Made?

Many products we buy and use were made in other countries. Do you have anything in your home made in another country? Was it bought there and brought to the United States, or did your family buy it here? Look at the labels on clothing, toys, foods, and other products. Make a list of all the countries that you find as sources for products. Mark each country on a world map. Think of ways to put the products into categories. Did more food products come from the Western Hemisphere? Did many items of clothing come from the continent of Asia? Did most toys come from China? Talk with your classmates about what you have discovered.

Know Your Rights

Get a copy of the Universal Declaration of Human Rights from the library or the Internet. Choose an article. For example, Article 1 reads: "All human beings are born free and equal in dignity and rights. They are endowed with reason and conscience and should act towards one another in a spirit of brotherhood." What do these words mean to you? Rewrite the article in your own words. Explain it to your classmates.

Use with *States and Regions*

Support for Language Development

1. Write in the letter of the picture and word that goes with the definition below.

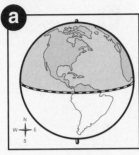
hemisphere

geography

environment

region

____ The study of the people and places of Earth

____ One half of Earth's surface

____ An area that is defined by certain features

____ All the surroundings and conditions that affect living things

2. Read the section called "Where, Why, and What." Then write the correct word or words to complete the sentences below.

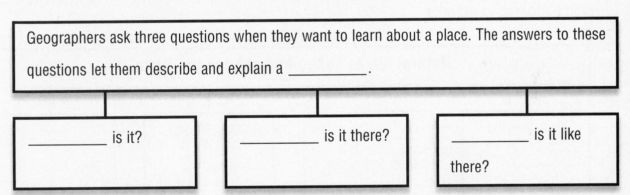

Geographers ask three questions when they want to learn about a place. The answers to these questions let them describe and explain a _____.

_____ is it?

_____ is it there?

_____ is it like there?

3. Match the words in the left column to the correct words in the right column.

A. Latitude and longitude lines

B. The study of the people and places of Earth is called

C. Geography helps us

D. Areas that share certain features are called

E. Geography

explains the processes that shape the land.

regions.

show the exact location of a place.

geography.

understand our environment.

Support for Language Development

1. Write the letter of the picture and word that goes with the definition below.

  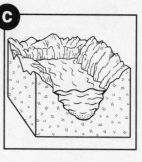 

| erosion | glacier | basin | tectonic plate |

____ A huge slab of slowly moving rock beneath the earth's crust

____ Process of wearing away rock and soil

____ An area with a low center surrounded by higher land

____ A huge mass of slowly moving ice

2. Read the sentences below. Write the correct word or words to complete each sentence.

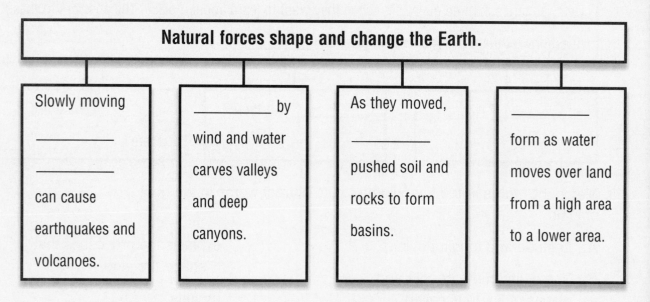

Natural forces shape and change the Earth.

Slowly moving _____ _____ can cause earthquakes and volcanoes.

_____ by wind and water carves valleys and deep canyons.

As they moved, _____ pushed soil and rocks to form basins.

_____ form as water moves over land from a high area to a lower area.

Use with *States and Regions*, pp. 16–19

Support for Language Development

1. Write in the letter of the picture and word that goes with the definition below.

product

natural resources

fossil fuel

renewable resources

nonrenewable resources

____ Things from the natural environment that people use

____ Things that the environment can replace after we use them

____ Things nature cannot replace after we use them

____ Something that is made from natural resources

____ An energy source formed by the remains of things that lived long ago

2. Read the section called "Using Resources Wisely." Write the correct word or words to complete each sentence below.

A. You can turn _____ when you leave a room.

B. You can use _____ when you brush your teeth.

C. You can _____ the _____, _____, and _____ you use.

Resources for Reaching All Learners
49
Use with *States and Regions*, pp. 24–29

Support for Language Development

1. Write the letter of the picture and word that goes with the definition below.

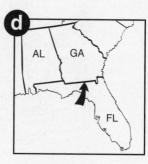

government   population   religion   boundary

____ the people who live in an area

____ a system of making and carrying out rules and laws

____ the edge of a region

____ a system of faith or worship

2. Read "One Place, Many Regions" on page 39 of your textbook. Look at the Venn diagram. Then fill in the blanks in the sentence below.

The city of Elizabeth is in both the region of _____

_____ and the region of _____.

New York City metropolitan area — Elizabeth — New Jersey

Support for Language Development

1. Write in the letters that go with the definitions below.

urban

suburban

rural

economy

agriculture

____ in country areas with fewer people and no large cities

____ the business of farming

____ in a city

____ in smaller towns near a city

____ the way the people in an area choose to use the area's resources

2. Choose three words from the word box on the right and write them under "Human Features" or "Natural Features" in the table.

Human Features	Natural Features
_____	_____
_____	_____
_____	_____

mountains	language
economy	wetlands
history	rivers

51
Use with *States and Regions*, pp. 42–45

Support for Language Development

1. Write the letter of the picture and word that goes with the definition below.

 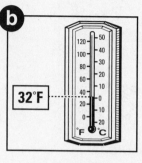  

precipitation   temperature   climate   elevation

____ the measure of how hot or cold the air is

____ water that falls to the earth as rain, snow, sleet, or hail

____ the height of the land

____ the usual weather conditions in a place over a long period of time

2. Read "Conditions and Climate" on page 53 of your textbook. Then fill in the blanks in the sentences with the correct word or words.

A. The _____ describes conditions like wind speed and direction, amount of moisture in the air, and _____.

B. _____ is the measure of how hot or cold the air is.

C. _____ is the usual weather conditions over a long period of time.

D. Three factors affect climate: _____, _____ from a major body of water, and _____.

Support for Language Development

1. Write the letter of the picture that goes with the definition below.

coast

coastal plain

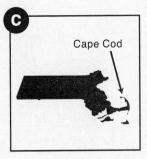

cape

bay

temperate

____ a point of land that sticks out into the water

____ land next to an ocean

____ without extremes

____ flat, level land next to a coast

____ a body of water partly surrounded by land but open to the sea

2. Reread "Land and Water of the East" on pages 72-73. Write the word or words that complete the sentences correctly.

   A. The East can be divided into two _____

   regions: mountains and _____ .

   B. The Appalachians were formed by the

   _____ of the earth.

   C. More people live on the coastal plain than in

   _____ .

   D. The land on _____ is less rugged than

   the mountains.

Use with *States and Regions*, pp. 72–75

Support for Language Development

1. Write the letter of the picture that goes with the definition below.

market economy

profit

factors of production

human resources

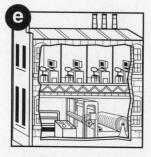

capital resources

____ the tools, machines, buildings, and other equipment a business uses to make goods or provide services

____ the people and materials needed to make goods or provide services

____ money left over after a business pays all its expenses

____ a system that lets people decide what to make, buy, and sell

____ the services, knowledge, skills, and intelligence that workers provide

2. Reread "Elements of Business" on page 82 of your textbook. There are 4 factors of production. Write one factor in each oval.

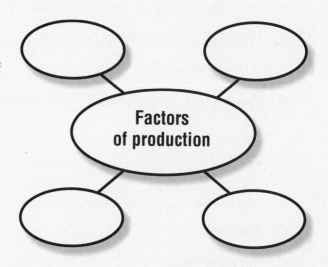

Factors of production

Support for Language Development

1. Write the letter of the picture that goes with the definition below.

culture

constitution

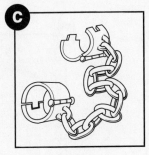

slavery

industry

immigration

_____ an unjust system in which one person owns another

_____ the movement from one nation to another

_____ the way of life of a particular group of people, including beliefs and values

_____ a business that makes goods in factories

_____ a plan for setting up and running a government

2. Reread "The Growth of Industries" on page 95 of your textbook. Write the word that correctly completes the sentence in the Solution box.

Problem

Immigrants from Europe wanted to escape war and poverty.

Solution

By the late 1800s, millions of people had _____ from Europe to the United States looking for factory jobs.

Resources for Reaching All Learners

55 Use with *States and Regions*, pp. 90–95

Support for Language Development

1. Write in the letter of the picture and word that goes with the definition below.

university

suburb

commuter

manufacturing

_____ A community that grows up outside of a larger city

_____ A school with several colleges that each focus on one area of study

_____ Making goods from other materials

_____ A person who travels between home and work every day

2. Write the correct word or words to complete the web below.

New England

Social Institutions:

Schools, places of worship,

_____

Tourism: historical sites,

skiing, swimming,

_____

Jobs: tourism, farming,

_____

Name _____ Date _____

Support for Language Development

1. Write the correct letter next to the definition.

judicial branch

skyscraper

governor

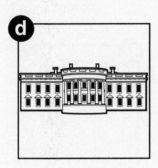

executive branch

legislative branch

____ A very tall building

____ The branch of government that makes the laws

____ The branch of government that makes sure the laws are put into action

____ The branch of government that explains the laws in courts

____ The head of the executive branch in the state government

2. Read the section of the lesson called "Public and Private Services."
Write the correct word or words to complete each sentence.

A. State governments are _____ institutions.

B. They serve communities within _____ borders.

C. Education, _____ and police protection, and highways

are all _____ services.

D. States pay for these services by collecting _____.

E. States tax the _____ people earn, the _____

they own, and the things they _____.

Use with *States and Regions*, pp. 114–117

Support for Language Development

1. Write the letter of the picture and word that goes with the definition below.

delta

b

adapt

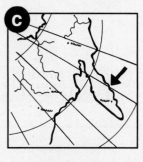

peninsula

interior

_____ A piece of land surrounded by water on three sides

_____ An area away from the coast or border

_____ A triangle-shaped area at the mouth of a river

_____ To change in order to better fit in an environment

2. Read the section of the lesson called "Climate and Wildlife." Then match the areas on the left to the correct descriptions on the right.

A. Ozark highlands   are usually warm

B. coastal areas   winters are mild

C. lowlands   can have severe weather

Use with *States and Regions*, pp. 132–135

Support for Language Development

1. Write the vocabulary word in the correct space.

| opportunity cost | producer | scarcity | consumer | dam |

_____   _____   _____

_____   _____

2. Write the vocabulary word or words that complete each sentence correctly.

A. _____ use water that runs through _____ to make electricity.

B. _____ buy this electricity.

C. _____ is when too few products are made for the number of consumers who want to buy them.

D. _____ is when you give up one thing in order to buy another.

Support for Language Development

1. Write the vocabulary word in the correct space.

| export | boycott | civil rights |

The rights that
every citizen has
by law

_____

A protest in which
people refuse to
do business with a
person or company

_____

A product that is
sent out of the
country to be sold
or traded

_____

2. Read "The Struggle for Civil Rights." Then read the sentences below. Write the correct word or words to complete each sentence.

Americans worked for equality and _____ _____ for all.

1920: Women won the right to _____.

1954: African Americans could go to the same _____ as whites.

1955: The law made _____ companies treat all passengers _____.

Support for Language Development

1. Write the letter of the picture and word that goes with the definition below.

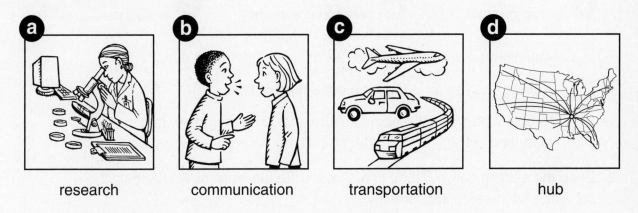

a — research b — communication c — transportation d — hub

_____ The business of carrying people or goods from one place to another

_____ A major center of activity

_____ To study something carefully to learn more about it

_____ The exchange of information

2. Read the section called "Things to Do." Why do people like to visit the Upper South? Write one activity in each box below.

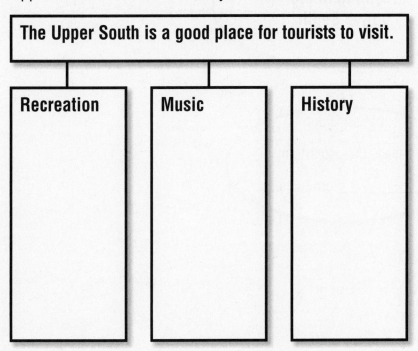

The Upper South is a good place for tourists to visit.

Recreation

Music

History

Name _____ Date _____

Support for Language Development

1. Write the letter of the word that goes with the definition below.

a ethnic group   **b** planned community   **c** pollution

_____ Anything that makes the land, water, or air impure or dirty

_____ A place to live that is mapped out ahead of time

_____ People who share the same culture, including language, music, food, and art

2. Read the section called "Rural Life." Then write the word or words that complete each sentence correctly.

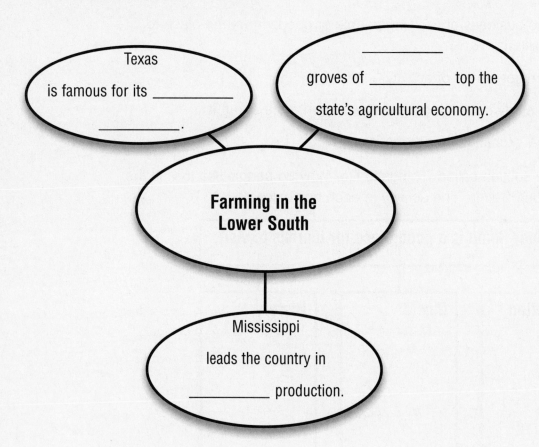

Texas is famous for its _____ _____.

_____ groves of _____ top the state's agricultural economy.

Farming in the Lower South

Mississippi leads the country in _____ production.

Support for Language Development

1. Write the letter of the picture and word that goes with the definition below.

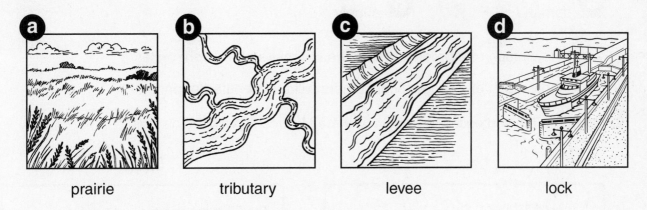

prairie   tributary   levee   lock

_____ part of a waterway that is closed off by gates

_____ a river or stream that flows into another river

_____ dry, mostly flat grassland with few trees

_____ a high river bank that stops the river from overflowing

2. Complete the sentences in the solution boxes.

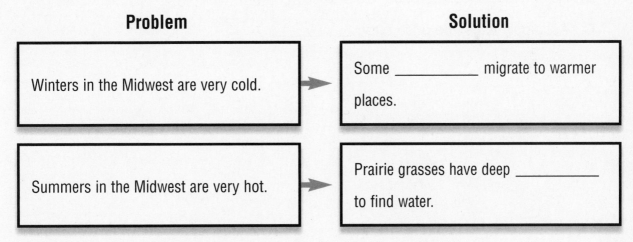

Problem

Winters in the Midwest are very cold.

Summers in the Midwest are very hot.

Solution

Some _____ migrate to warmer places.

Prairie grasses have deep _____ to find water.

3. Write the word or words that complete the sentence correctly.

A. The Midwest lies between the _____

_____ and the Rocky Mountains.

B. In the Midwest, summers are hot and there are terrible

windstorms called _____.

Use with *States and Regions,* pp. 190–193

Name _____ Date _____

Support for Language Development

1. Write the letter of the word that goes with the definition below.

a demand   **b** supply

____ How much of a product producers will make at different prices

____ How much of a product consumers will buy at different prices

2. Complete the sentences to explain why the Midwest developed as it did.

Cause   **Effect**

| The Midwest has rich _____ and plenty of rainfall. | → | The Midwest became a major farming region. |

3. Read "Supply and Demand" on page 199 of your textbook. Write the missing words in the sentences below.

A. Supply and _____ affect each other.

B. As demand rises, the price tends to _____.

C. As supply rises, the price often _____.

Support for Language Development

1. Write the letter of the word that goes with the definition below.

a homestead   **b** reservation   **c** assembly line

____ a piece of land given to someone to settle and farm there

____ land set aside by the government for American Indians

____ a way of manufacturing goods where each worker does one small part of the job

2. Write the word or words that complete the sentence correctly.

A. Thomas Jefferson bought the _____

_____ from France in 1803.

B. Many _____ and _____ immigrated to

the Midwest.

C. The Homestead Act of 1862 gave land to people who would live

there for _____ _____.

Resources for Reaching All Learners
65   **Use with *States and Regions*, pp. 204–209**

Name _____ Date _____

Support for Language Development

1. Circle the word that goes with the definition.

a railway that runs above the ground on raised tracks

elevation chain   celebrated train   elevator   elevated train

the payments for work

wags   wedges   wages   warns

2. Read "Living in Chicago, Illinois" on page 219 of your textbook. Then write the word or words that complete the sentences correctly.

A. Chicago has _____ people than any other city in the

Great Lakes States.

B. Chicago's location near important waterways helped it become a

major _____ center.

C. As Chicago grew, public _____ became necessary

to take workers to and from downtown.

Name _____ Date _____

Support for Language Development

1. Write the vocabulary word on the line next to its meaning.

population density	grain elevator

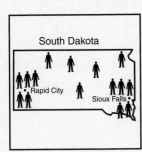 	_____	a measure of how many people live in an area
	_____	a building used to store wheat or other grains

2. Read "Rural Lands on the Plains" on page 230 of your textbook. Complete the sentences by putting in the missing words.

A. Miles of _____ land separate many cities and towns in the _____ States.

B. Much of the Plains States was once a vast _____.

C. People plowed the land, which is now used for growing _____ and grazing _____.

Support for Language Development

1. Write in the letters that go with the definitions below.

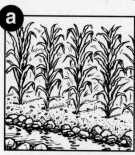

irrigation

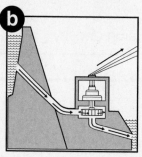

hydroelectric power

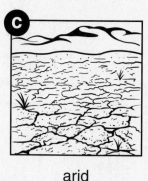

arid

____ electricity produced from flowing
water

____ very dry

____ a way of supplying land with
water

2. Read "Water, Climate, and Wildlife" on page 248 of your textbook.
Then write the word or words that complete the sentence correctly.

A. The Pacific Ocean affects _____ in the West.

B. Air from the Pacific gives the _____ coast

_____ rain than the southern coast.

C. The air stays dry as it flows down eastern mountains. This makes

the climate there _____.

3. Read "Mountains in the West" on page
247 of your textbook. Draw a line from
the landform to the word that tells how
it was formed.

Rocky Mountains	Rivers
Cascade Mountains	Tectonic plates
Yosemite Valley	Glaciers
Grand Canyon	Volcanoes

68
Use with *States and Regions*, pp. 246–249

Support for Language Development

1. Write in the letters of the picture that go with the definitions below.

national park

specialization

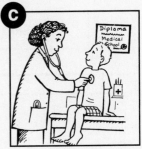

skilled worker

____ an area of land set aside by the federal government

____ when a business makes only a few goods or provides just one service

____ someone who has special training or education to do a job

2. Read "Using Resources" on page 256 of your textbook. Then write the names of things that people grow or make from the natural resources in the West.

Soil	Trees	Ocean

3. Write the word or words that complete the sentence correctly.

A. A company that makes one part of a car, not the whole car, is

practicing _____.

B. Many people in the computer industry have advanced training.

They are _____.

Name _____ Date _____

Support for Language Development

1. Write the vocabulary word on the line next to its meaning.

mission	wagon train	transcontinental railroad

	_____	train system that linked the East and the West
	_____	a settlement for teaching religion to local people
	_____	a line of wagons that carried settlers and their belongings

2. Read "Spanish Settlements" on page 264 of your textbook. Fill in the missing words.

Causes

Spanish soldiers hoped to find gold.

As they moved into Indian land, they came into _____ with the Indians who lived there.

Effects

They traveled north and made a _____ at Santa Fe.

They used _____ to take Indian land.

Name _____ Date _____

Support for Language Development

1. Match each definition to its correct picture and word.

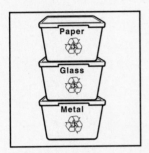

conservation

The breakdown of rock caused by wind, water, and weather

weathering

Using something carefully and not wasting it

2. Read the section of the lesson called "Using Water." Then read the sentences below. Use the correct words to complete the sentence.

Problem

There are only a few rivers. They are often overused.

Solution

Rivers have been _____ to

create _____ .

3. Match the state on the left with a sentence that best describes it on the right.

Arizona   Some areas of this state only get 4 inches of rain a year.

New Mexico   Tourists come to visit the natural arches in this state.

Nevada   The largest city in the Southwest is in this state.

Utah   Most pueblos on the Rio Grande are in this state.

Support for Language Development

1. Write the letter of the picture and word that goes with the definition below.

     ecosystem   habitat   extinct

_____ An environment and all its living things, working together as a unit

_____ No longer existing

_____ The natural home of a plant or animal

2. Read "Cities and Rural Areas." Then compare life in the urban and rural areas of the Mountain States. Use the phrases in the box to complete the diagram.

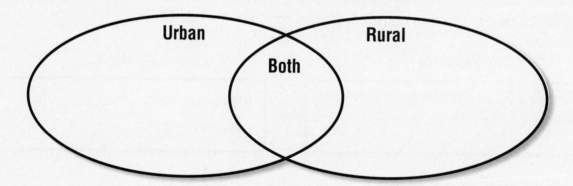

Urban   Rural

Both

few people
enjoy outdoor activities
are centers of industry,
    entertainment, and health care

raise sheep and cattle
travel to get supplies and services
many people

Name _____ Date _____

Support for Language Development

1. Write the vocabulary word next to its meaning.

| migrant worker   seasonal |

_____ happening at certain times of the year

_____ a worker who moves from place to place to find seasonal work

2. Read "Agriculture Activities" in your textbook. Draw a line to connect the region in the boxes on the left to the kinds of crops grown in the boxes on the right.

| cool, wet coastal regions | wheat and sugar beets |

| east of the Cascade Mountains | pineapples |

| Southern California | peas, broccoli, pears, apples, and strawberries |

| Hawaii | citrus fruits, almonds, figs, and kiwi |

Name _____ Date _____

Support for Language Development

1. Write the letter of the picture and word that go with the definitions below.

citizen

democracy

representative

election

constitution

_____ the way voters choose people to serve in government

_____ a system in which the people hold the power of government

_____ a person who acts for a group of people

_____ a person born in a country or who promises to be loyal to the country

_____ a plan for setting up and running a government

2. Read "The Constitution" on page 310 of your textbook. Write two phrases that tell what the Constitution and the Bill of Rights do.

Our Constitution and Bill of Rights:

try to ensure liberty, equality, and justice for all		

Name _____ Date _____

Support for Language Development

1. Write the letter of the word that goes with the definition below.

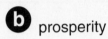 **a** interdependence   **b** prosperity 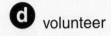 **c** heritage **d** volunteer

____ someone who agrees to provide a service without pay

____ a relationship in which people depend on each other

____ traditions that people have honored for many years

____ wealth and success

2. Read "Linking Regions" on page 314 of your textbook. The United States is linked by several communications systems. Find some examples in the text or think of others. Write their names in the small ovals.

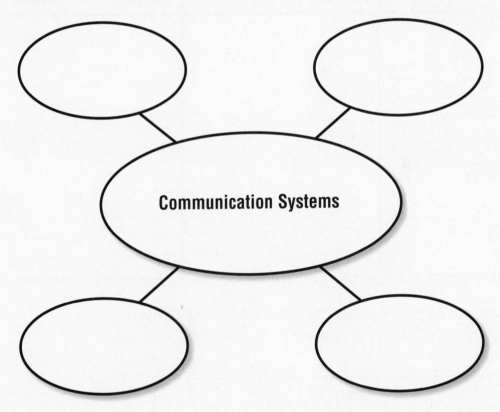

Communication Systems

Name _____ Date _____

Support for Language Development

1. Write the vocabulary word on the line next to its meaning.

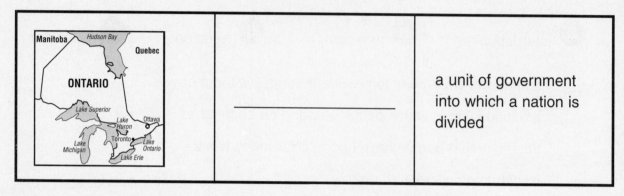

	_____	a unit of government into which a nation is divided

2. Canada and Mexico both border the United States, but they are very different. Fill in the chart with information about each country.

Feature	Canada	Mexico
Climate	_____	_____
Mountain ranges	_____	_____
Other landforms	_____	_____
Language	_____	_____

3. Look at the map on page 321 of your textbook. Fill in the following chart with the names of the three largest countries in North America.

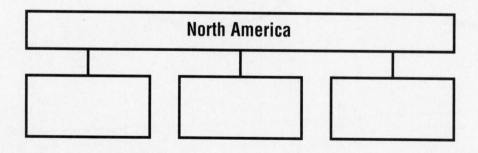

North America

Support for Language Development

1. Write the vocabulary word on the line next to its meaning.

rain forest	isthmus

_____

a narrow strip of land that connects two larger land areas

_____

dense forest that gets large amounts of rainfall every year

2. Look at the words in the box below. Read pages 329–331 of your textbook and circle the words when you find them. Then write the words in the right place in the diagram. If the word is found only in Central America, write it in the circle on the left. If it is only found in South America, write it in the circle on the right. If it is found in both Central and South America, put it under "Both" in the overlapping middle area of both circles.

canal
rain forest
volcanoes
Mayan Empire
Andes Mountains
Inca

Central America   **Both**   **South America**

Name _____ Date _____

Support for Language Development

1. Circle the word that goes with the definition.

the kinds of plants that grow in a region

vegetarian   vegetation   vegetable   verification

a regional form of a language

delete   direct   dialect   dilate

2. Read the section called "Types of Regions." Match each kind of region to its description.

climate region	Most of the northern part of North America is forested.
landform region	The Himalaya Mountains stretch across Asia.
language region	Most people in Egypt practice the religion Islam.
cultural region	The tropics are wet and warm all year long.
vegetation region	People in Spain, France, and Italy speak similar languages.

Resources for Reaching All Learners

78

Use with *States and Regions*, pp. 340–343

Support for Language Development

1. Write the letter of the picture and word that goes with each definition below.

ally   treaty   alliance

import   free enterprise

_____ a country or group that joins with another country or group for a common purpose

_____ a system that lets people control their own businesses and decide what goods to buy

_____ an agreement between allies to seek a common goal

_____ an official document that defines an agreement between nations

_____ a product brought in from another country.

2. Read the following sentences. Write a T in front of the sentences that are true. Write an F in front of the sentences that are false.

_____ **A.** The United States only trades with countries that have a free enterprise system.

_____ **B.** International trade is an important part of our economy.

_____ **C.** The United States has rules to protect some industries.

Use with *States and Regions*, pp. 348–351

Support for Language Development

1. Write the vocabulary word on the line next to its meaning.

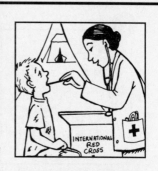

_____ a group that is not part of a national government

_____ a set of basic rules to which the United States and many other countries have agreed

2. Read the section called "The United Nations" in your textbook. Draw a line to connect the name of the UN organization or document to what it does.

The World Health Organization	helps countries build their economies.
The Universal Declaration of Human Rights	helps improve health conditions around the world.
The World Bank	protects the basic rights of people in all countries.

80 Use with *States and Regions*, pp. 354–357

Answers

Name _____ Date _____

Summary: Land and Water

Before You Read
Find and underline each vocabulary word.

Major Landforms
Natural forces shape and change the earth. Some natural forces take place underground. Slowly moving tectonic plates cause earthquakes and volcanoes. Melted rock from volcanoes can form mountains. Volcanoes created the Cascade Mountains in the northwest United States. The Rocky Mountains in the western part of North America were formed when tectonic plates pushed together. The tectonic plates broke and moved rocks deep in the earth's crust.

Land is also shaped by erosion. Wind and water carve valleys and deep canyons in rock. Wind can also blow soil away. Erosion rounded the Appalachian Mountains that run from Maine to Alabama in the eastern United States. Glaciers once covered parts of North America. They pushed soil and rocks as they moved. Moving glaciers also caused erosion. They helped shape hills, valleys, and plains.

Bodies of Water
Moving glaciers scooped soil and rocks to form basins. When the glaciers melted, some water stayed in these basins. This is how the five Great Lakes were created.

Lakes form when water enters a low area faster than it can leave. Some lakes drain out through rivers. Some water seeps into the ground. Some water evaporates into the air. The only way water can leave Utah's Great Salt Lake is by evaporating. Minerals left behind make the water salty.

Rivers form as water moves over high land to lower land. Small streams flow into larger ones. Larger streams flow into rivers. Rivers flow into the ocean. The Mississippi River is the longest in North America. It starts in Minnesota and drains into the Gulf of Mexico. Many other rivers flow into the Mississippi. The Mississippi is one of the world's busiest shipping routes.

People have always settled near rivers. Rivers bring water for drinking and farming. Rivers provide transportation. Flowing water runs machines.

tectonic plate *noun*, a huge slab of slowly moving rock beneath the earth's crust
erosion *noun*, a process of wearing away rock and soil
glacier *noun*, a huge mass of slowly moving ice
basin *noun*, an area with a low center surrounded by higher land

After You Read
REVIEW **What forces can shape the land?** Highlight six forces that can shape the land.
REVIEW **In what way did glaciers create the Great Lakes?** As glaciers moved, they scooped up soil and rocks. What did this create? Draw a box around the paragraph that tells the answer.

Name _____ Date _____

Summary: The Geography of Our World

Before You Read
Find and underline each vocabulary word.

Welcome to Geography
Geography is the study of the people and places of Earth. It explains forces that shape the land. Geographers study how our environment affects us and how we affect our environment. Geographers ask three questions about a place. They ask, "Where is it?" If you want to tell someone where you live, you can say your address or you can say where your home is in relation to other places. Geographers ask, "Why is it there?" They look for clues about forces that shaped mountains, rivers, landforms, and bodies of water.

Geographers study why some communities grow and some disappear. They ask "What is it like there?" They study the physical features of the land. They also study human features, such as how people use land, the work they do, their foods, languages, and beliefs.

Where in the World Are You?
A globe shows the earth's oceans and continents. Continents are masses of land. There are four large oceans: the Atlantic, Arctic, Pacific, and Indian. There are seven continents: Africa, Antarctica, Asia, Australia, Europe, North America, and South America. The earth can be divided into hemispheres. The United States is in the Northern and Western Hemispheres. The United States has many regions. A region is an area that can be described by features, such as the language people speak there or the kinds of landforms found there.

Maps with latitude and longitude lines show the exact location of a place. Latitude lines run parallel to the equator. Lines of longitude, also called meridians, run from the North Pole to the South Pole. The lines have numbers, called degrees. The equator is 0 degrees latitude. It divides Earth into two hemispheres, Northern and Southern. Other latitude lines are measured in degrees north or south. The prime meridian is 0 degrees longitude. Other longitude lines are measured in degrees east or west. To give the exact location of a place, find where the latitude and longitude lines cross. For example, New Orleans is at 30 degrees north, 90 degrees west. This is written as 30° N, 90° W.

geography *noun*, the study of the people and places of Earth
environment *noun*, all the surroundings and conditions that affect living things
hemisphere *noun*, one half of the earth's surface
region *noun*, an area that is defined by certain features

After You Read
REVIEW **What are two ways to describe the location of a place?** Highlight the sentence that tells how you can describe where you live.
REVIEW **What physical features does a globe show?** Draw a box around the sentence that tells what features are shown on a globe.
REVIEW **Why are maps useful?** What does a map with latitude and longitude lines show? Underline the sentence that tells the answer.

Answers *continued*

Name _____ Date _____

Summary: What Is a Region?

Before You Read
Find and underline each vocabulary word.

government *noun,* a system of making and carrying out rules and laws
population *noun,* the people who live in an area
religion *noun,* a system of faith or worship
boundary *noun,* the edge of a region

Defining Regions

The world can be divided into regions. A region is an area that shares one or more features. These features make regions different from one another. People use regions to organize their ideas about places and people. For example, a farming region is different from a fishing region. A farming region in Europe may grow different crops than a farming region in Asia.

Countries and states are regions that have the same government. Other regions are based on landforms or the plants or animals that live there. Regions can be based on the population. People may share a religion or language. Regions take up space or land. Some regions have borders to show exactly where they begin and end. Countries and states have borders that show exactly what land area they contain. Other regions have a boundary. Some boundaries, like rivers, are natural. Some are man-made, such as a road.

After You Read

REVIEW What kind of region has borders?
Underline the sentence that tells which regions have borders.

How Regions Are Used

Creating regions helps people to understand and organize large spaces. Governments divide their countries or states into regions. Government leaders gather facts about the people, environment, and natural resources in each region. They use this information to decide how to use resources and give services to people who need them.

People use regions to make decisions. Business leaders use information about regions to decide if they want to open a store or sell a product there. For example, a company that makes coats looks for regions with cold weather.

Regions can overlap. The same place can be in more than one region. For example, the city of Elizabeth is in the state of New Jersey. It is also in the New York metropolitan region, because it is close to that city. It is also in the East, a region of the United States.

REVIEW In what ways do people use regions to make decisions? Draw a box around two sentences that tell how the government and business leaders use regions to decide what to do.

4   Use with *States and Regions*, pp. 36–39

Name _____ Date _____

Summary: Resources of the United States

Before You Read
Find and underline each vocabulary word.

natural resources *noun,* things from the natural environment that people use
renewable resources *noun,* things that the environment can replace after we use them
nonrenewable resources *noun,* things nature cannot replace after we use them
product *noun,* something that is made from natural resources
fossil fuel *noun,* an energy source formed by the remains of things that lived long ago

A Land of Rich Resources

Natural resources are things from the natural environment that people use. The first Americans used natural resources, such as water, soil, plants, and animals. Food, clothing, houses, and fuel all come from natural resources. Trees and other living things are renewable resources. Soil is renewable if it is used carefully. Minerals like copper and iron are nonrenewable resources. They were formed over millions of years. Once we use them up, they will be gone forever. Sunlight, wind, and water are flow resources. We can use their energy as they move through the environment.

After You Read

REVIEW What is a natural resource? Highlight the sentence that tells the answer.

Using Natural Resources

Rich soil covers much of the land in the United States. People use soil to raise crops and livestock. There are great forests in North America. People cut trees to make wood and paper products. The oceans are a source of seafood. Rivers provide transportation routes and their flow generates power. We use water for drinking and farming.

Miners dig for mineral resources, such as metals and stone. People use natural resources to make energy. We use energy for electricity, heat, and transportation. Most of our energy comes from burning fossil fuels, such as coal, oil, and natural gas. The United States produces much of the world's fossil fuels. It also uses more fuel than any other country. Fossil fuels are nonrenewable resources.

REVIEW Why are natural resources important to the people of the United States? Highlight ways that people in the United States use natural resources.

Using Resources Wisely

People are finding other energy resources. The sun's power and heat from within the earth are used to make energy. Wind and water are used to make electricity. Nuclear energy uses natural resources, but it causes safety problems.

People do not always use natural resources wisely. People dump waste into water, burn fuels that harm the air, cut too many trees, and take too many fish. You can help to protect natural resources by using less energy and recycling.

REVIEW How can you help protect natural resources? Circle the sentence that tells what you can do to protect natural resources.

3   Use with *States and Regions*, pp. 24–29

Answers

Name _____ Date _____

Summary: Climate Regions

Before You Read
Find and underline each vocabulary word.

precipitation *noun*, water that falls to the earth as rain, snow, sleet, or hail

temperature *noun*, a measure of how hot or cold the air is

climate *noun*, the usual weather conditions in a place over a long period of time

elevation *noun*, the height of the land

After You Read

REVIEW **What causes daily changes in the weather?** Underline the sentence that tells what causes weather conditions to change.

REVIEW **What factors are used to divide the United States into climate regions and subregions?** Circle the sentence that tells what climate regions are based on.

REVIEW **In what ways are people affected by extreme weather events?** Draw a box around the sentence that tells what extreme weather does to people and their surroundings.

Weather and Climate

Weather is the day-to-day conditions in the atmosphere. Air movement causes weather conditions to change. Weather conditions are factors like wind speed and direction, precipitation, and temperature. Weather conditions determine the <u>climate</u> of a region. Climate is the usual weather conditions in a place over a long period of time.

Three things affect climate. The first is latitude. Places far from the equator get less heat from the sun and are colder. Places closer to an ocean have a smaller change in temperature between seasons. Third, the elevation of a region affects temperature.

A Land of Many Climates

The United States has six climate regions. (They are based on <u>temperature and precipitation.</u>) Tropical regions are warm all year. Hawaii is in a tropical wet subregion. Dry regions get little precipitation. The region near the Rocky Mountains is dry. The mild mid-latitude regions have hot summers and mild winters. California is in this region.

Severe mid-latitude climates in the middle of the United States have cold winters. Polar regions such as Northern Alaska are colder year-round. The highland climate region is in the mountains, which are cooler and wetter than the lower land around them.

Climate and People

Climate affects how people live. People heat or cool their houses. People in dry regions must use water carefully to have enough to drink and water crops.

Climate also affects the economy. In Maine or Alaska, the growing season is short, so people cannot farm all year long. But California has two growing seasons, and farming is very important to the economy.

Extreme weather, like hurricanes, tornadoes, and blizzards, can destroy buildings and crops. Burning fossil fuels may be changing weather patterns by warming the earth.

Name _____ Date _____

Summary: Regions of the United States

Before You Read
Find and underline each vocabulary word.

urban *adjective*, in a city

suburban *adjective*, in smaller towns near a city

rural *adjective*, in country areas with fewer people and no large cities

economy *noun*, the way the people of an area choose to use the area's resources

agriculture *noun*, the business of farming

After You Read

REVIEW **Over time, what might happen to regions that are based on human features?** Underline two sentences that tell what happens when populations change.

REVIEW **Why does each state belong to a certain region?** Draw a box around three sentences that tell how states are linked in a region.

Types of Regions

The United States has many regions. One way people define regions is by physical features, such as landforms or water systems. The United States has mountain regions, valleys, plateaus, and plains. Other regions include wetlands, grasslands, forests, and deserts. Regions can also be defined by human features, such as religion or language. <u>Over time, as the population changes, the region may also change. The region may grow or shrink.</u>

Regions can also be defined by the work people do. For example, parts of Kansas are in the Wheat Belt, a region where many farmers grow wheat. The Silicon Valley in California is a region where many people work at computer jobs.

Other regions can be defined by the kinds of communities people live in. Cities are <u>urban</u> regions. The smaller towns around cities are called <u>suburban.</u> Together, cities and suburban cities are called metropolitan regions. Country areas are <u>rural.</u> They do not have cities or many people.

States and Regions

In this book, the United States is divided into four major regions: the East, the South, the Midwest, and the West. They are named for their geographic location. Each region includes several states that are close together. States in a region share natural features. They may have similar landforms or animals. For example, states in the West use the same rivers to water their farmland.

Human features also link the states in each region. Much of the land in the West was once controlled by Spain and Mexico. The states in the West share a common history. States in a region are also linked by their economy. In the South, agriculture and factories are important for the economy. Many people work on farms or in factories. Some regions are linked to a special feature, like a major city or favorite sports team. These ideas are a small part of what makes up a region.

Answers continued

Name _____ Date _____

Summary: Resources and Economy

Natural Resources of the East

People in the East use natural resources to get the things they want and to make goods to sell. People mine coal in the Appalachian Mountains. The coal is used to make electricity. Granite and marble from Maine and Vermont are used to make buildings. Forests are cut down to make houses, paper, furniture, and fuel. Many fruits and vegetables are grown in the East. Maine farmers grow blueberries and potatoes. Cranberries are grown in sandy marshes in New Jersey and Massachusetts. The Atlantic Ocean is an important resource for fish and shellfish.

Working in the East

The United States has a market economy. People can start almost any business. They can decide what to make, how to make it, and how to sell it. They keep the profit after they pay for materials, labor, and other costs. This is different than a command economy. In a command economy, the government decides what to make, who will make it, and who will get it.

People trade resources or money for goods. When people trade a lot the economy grows. Businesses use trade to get the resources they need. Moving goods is part of trade. Trucks move raw materials to factories and finished products to stores.

Some businesses make goods, such as chemicals, medicines, machinery, and clothing. Then they sell the goods. Other businesses perform services that people want. Lawyers, plumbers, and banks sell services.

Elements of Business

Businesses use human resources and capital resources to make things. They need people, equipment, and some raw materials. These are called factors of production. Entrepreneurs use these to start and own businesses. In our market economy, we have private ownership. This means that business owners make decisions and earn profits. Individual people, not the government, own the factors of production.

Before You Read
Find and underline each vocabulary word.

market economy *noun*, a system that lets people decide what to make, buy, and sell

profit *noun*, money left over after a business pays all its expenses

factors of production *noun*, the people and materials needed to make goods or provide services

human resources *noun*, the services, knowledge, skills, and intelligence that workers provide

capital resources *noun*, the tools, machines, buildings, and other equipment a business uses to make goods or provide services

After You Read

REVIEW Why is the farmland of the East an important natural resource? Underline crops farmers grow in the East.

REVIEW How is making goods different from performing services? Draw a box around the paragraph that tells the answer.

REVIEW Why is private ownership important in a market economy? Circle the sentence that tells what owners of a business do.

Name _____ Date _____

Summary: Land and Climate

Land and Water of the East

The region between the coast of the Atlantic Ocean and the Great Lakes is called the East. It includes six New England States and five Mid-Atlantic states. The East has mountains and plains. It also has many lakes and rivers.

The Appalachian Mountains stretch from Maine to Alabama. They were formed millions of years ago when two continents collided. Wind and weather wore the mountains down. Glaciers made valleys in the mountains.

The coastal plain is east of the Appalachians. In New England, the coastal plain is mostly underwater. The coastal plain is wider from Massachusetts to Florida. People built big cities, farms, and factories on the coastal plain. More people live there than in the mountains. The land is less rough and it is closer to water routes. In the mountains people farm, mine coal, and cut trees.

The East is a land of lakes, rivers, and ocean. Glaciers formed many lakes. Rocks and sand left by glaciers also formed islands and capes. People built settlements near the best bays along the coast. Ships from other continents carried people and goods into these harbors along the coast. Boats could come inland on big rivers. Some of the rivers had waterfalls. People learned to use the waterfalls to power machines.

Climate and Its Effects

The East is about halfway between the North Pole and the equator. The East's location affects its climate. The climate is temperate. It is not too cold or too hot. There are four seasons. Winters are snowy and cold. Summers are warm and humid. It rains or snows during the four seasons.

The ocean affects the coastal climate. Cool breezes blow from the sea on hot days, and warm breezes blow on cold days. The climate affects the people, animals, and plants that live there. People change with the seasons. Animals' food supplies change with the seasons. Squirrels bury nuts to dig up in winter. Bears and other animals hibernate. They sleep for up to 100 days. Trees like maples and oaks drop their leaves each winter to survive the lack of water.

Before You Read
Find and underline each vocabulary word.

coast *noun*, land that borders an ocean

coastal plain *noun*, flat, level land next to a coast

cape *noun*, a point of land that sticks out into the water

bay *noun*, a body of water partly surrounded by land but open to the sea

temperate *adjective*, without extremes

After You Read

REVIEW Why are more cities built on the coastal plain than in the mountains? Circle the words that tell about land in the mountains.

REVIEW In what ways does the climate of the East affect the people, animals, and plants that live there? Draw a box around 6 sentences that tell what people, animals, and trees do to live in the climate.

Answers

Name _____ Date _____

Summary: What's Special About New England

Before You Read
Find and underline each vocabulary word.

suburb *noun,* a community that grows up outside of a larger city

university *noun,* a school with several colleges that each focus on one area of study

manufacturing *noun,* making goods from other materials

commuter *noun,* a person who travels between home and work every day

After You Read

REVIEW **What kinds of social institutions did the Puritans build?** Circle two social institutions that were started by the Puritans.

REVIEW **In what ways do rural New Englanders make a living?** Highlight sentences that tell about the work people who live in rural areas do.

Where People Live

There are six states in New England: Connecticut, Maine, Massachusetts, New Hampshire, Rhode Island, and Vermont. The biggest city is Boston in Massachusetts. It has a big harbor. Boston was once a major shipping center. Now, Boston is a center for banking and insurance. There are factories that make goods and high-tech products. Publishing and printing are important industries.

In the mid-1800s, many immigrants from Ireland moved to Boston. Many Italian people came to Boston in the late 1800s. After World War I, many African Americans moved from the South to Boston. Immigrants from Europe, Asia, Latin America, and Africa have come to live in Boston and the suburbs around it. Some of these people work in the city. They have to drive to work or take the subway. Boston was the first U.S. city to build a subway.

The Puritans who founded the city created strong social institutions. They built the first (free school) and Harvard, the first American (college). It became a university. Religion was an important subject in these schools. Puritans wanted their children to learn to read the Bible. Today, there are many schools, universities, and places of worship in Boston.

Rural New England

Rural New England includes New Hampshire, Vermont, and Maine. Most people in rural areas work in service industries, such as tourism. Some work in manufacturing. Many workers are commuters who work in nearby cities. There are farmers in New England. The soil is rocky and the growing season is short. Most New England farmers grow one crop or raise dairy cows.

Many people travel to New England for their vacations. Tourists like to visit historical places. They go skiing in the mountains or swim at the beach. Some tourists go to festivals.

Name _____ Date _____

Summary: People of the East

Before You Read
Find and underline each vocabulary word.

culture *noun,* the way of life of a particular group of people, including beliefs and values

constitution *noun,* a plan for setting up and running a government

slavery *adjective,* an unjust system in which one person owns another

industry *noun,* a business that makes goods in factories

immigration *noun,* the movement from one nation to another

After You Read

REVIEW **How did climate and natural resources affect American Indian cultures in the past?** Draw a box around sentences that tell how Indians lived.

REVIEW **In what ways did the East change after Europeans arrived?** Underline the sentence that tells how the Europeans affected the Indians who lived there.

REVIEW **What caused many immigrants to come to the United States in the late 1800s?** Highlight the sentence that tells why people left Europe and came to America.

First Peoples

American Indians have lived in the East for thousands of years. Each group's culture was affected by climate and natural resources. Indian nations used resources differently. The Haudenosaunee, who are also called the Iroquois, built houses, tools, weapons, and canoes with wood from the forests. In the north, the growing season was short, so the Micmac hunted for food. Further south, the growing season was longer. The Lenni Lenape grew corn and tobacco. They farmed in the summer and hunted in the winter. Today, American Indians in the East have a modern lifestyle, but preserve their culture.

Colonies and Traders

Explorers from Europe came to North America in the 1500s. In the 1600s, Pilgrims and Puritans came to practice their religion freely. England started colonies in the East along the coast. The Dutch settled in the Hudson River Valley. Along the St. Lawrence River, the French traded pots, cloth, and tools for furs from the Indians.

More Europeans came. They built towns and farms. They forced the Indians from most of their land. By the late 1700s, many American colonists wanted to be free from England. They fought the British and won independence. The new nation's constitution provided a written plan for the country's new government. Europeans had brought captives from Africa to the Americas and enslaved them. Most enslaved Africans worked in the South. Some traders in the East grew rich from this business of slavery. Ship building was another important business.

Factories and Workers

By the end of the 1700s, new inventions changed life for workers. A new spinning machine and power loom helped make the textile industry grow. Many young women came from farms to work in the textile industry. Cities grew as immigration increased. In the late 1800s, millions of people fled war and poverty in Europe and came to find jobs in American factories. Many African Americans also moved north to work in factories.

Answers continued

Name _____ Date _____

Summary: Land and Climate

Before You Read
Find and underline each vocabulary word.

peninsula *noun*, a piece of land surrounded by water on three sides
interior *adjective*, an area away from the coast or border
delta *noun*, a triangle-shaped area at the mouth of a river
adapt *verb*, to change in order to better fit in an environment

Land and Water of the South

There are fourteen states in the South. The region is divided into the Upper South and the Lower South. The Upper South has high flat areas called plateaus. Some states have rolling hills and rich river valleys. Some states in the Lower South are at sea level. They have beaches, swamps, and wetlands.

The coastline of the South includes both the Atlantic Ocean and the Gulf of Mexico. These coastal plains are the lowlands. The Gulf coastal plain stretches from the Rio Grande in Texas to the tip of the Florida peninsula. The Atlantic coastal plain stretches from Florida along the Atlantic Ocean to Virginia. The Appalachian Mountains and the Ozark Plateau are in the interior. They are the South's highest landforms.

The Mississippi River carries fertile soil to the huge delta at the Gulf of Mexico. There are also other wetlands in the South. Cities in the South grew near rivers or coasts. People use water to travel and move goods.

Climate and Wildlife

The South is closer to the equator and tends to be warmer and moister than northern regions. It also has a longer growing season. Southern farmers can grow crops for most of the year.

The South has more than one climate. The latitude, elevation, and closeness to the water affect climate. These factors can be different in each state. The ocean keeps temperatures in coastal areas warm. Winters can be mild and summers can be hot and humid. It is colder in the hills and plateaus. In the Ozark highlands there are often storms and tornados. Tropical storms and hurricanes cause flooding and other damage in the South every year.

Plants and animals have adapted to the Southern climate. In Florida, mangrove trees live in salty swamps. Along the coast, sea turtles hide their eggs on beaches above the high tide line.

After You Read

REVIEW In what ways is the Gulf coastal plain different from the Ozark Plateau? Highlight sentences that tell about each region.

REVIEW Why does the South have such a variety of climates? Underline the sentence that tells about latitude and elevation.

12   Use with *States and Regions*, pp. 132–135

Name _____ Date _____

Summary: What's Special About the Mid-Atlantic Region

Before You Read
Find and underline each vocabulary word.

skyscraper *noun*, a very tall building
legislative branch *noun*, the branch of government that makes the laws
executive branch *noun*, the branch of government that makes sure the laws are put into action
judicial branch *noun*, the branch of government that interprets, or explains, the laws in courts
governor *noun*, the head of the executive branch in the state government

Where People Live

The Mid-Atlantic region contains New York, New Jersey, Maryland, Delaware, Pennsylvania, and Washington, D.C. There are many big cities in this region. New York City is the largest city in the nation. It was built at the mouth of the Hudson River. Ships from Europe sailed into the big harbor. European settlers used the river to move resources and goods from inland North America to Europe. Trade developed. The city spread out to include Brooklyn, Queens, Staten Island, and the Bronx. People come to New York from all over the world. New York City has skyscrapers. It is a world center for publishing, advertising, and technology. Millions of tourists visit New York every year. They enjoy museums and plays. They visit famous places like the Statue of Liberty.

Suburbs surround the cities in the Mid-Atlantic region. People moved to the suburbs because the cities became crowded. There are many farms in the Mid-Atlantic region. Farms produce dairy products, chickens, and flowers. Coal is mined in Pennsylvania. Tourists ski on the mountains and swim at the beaches. They also visit Washington, D.C., the nation's capital.

State Governments

Each state in the United States has its own constitution and government. The government is in the capital city. State governments have three branches. The legislative branch makes the laws. The executive branch makes sure the laws are put into action. The governor of the state is the head of the executive branch. The judicial branch explains the laws in courts. State governments are public institutions. They provide education, fire and police protection, and highways for people in the state. They pay for these services by collecting taxes. People can be taxed on the property they own, the purchases they make, or the money they earn.

After You Read

REVIEW Why was New York's location important to its growth? What did European settlers use the river for? What was the result? Draw boxes around the sentences that tell you the answers.

REVIEW What are the three branches of state government and what do they do? Highlight the three branches of government. Underline the sentences that tell what each branch is responsible for.

11   Use with *States and Regions*, pp. 114–117

Use with *States and Regions*

Answers

Name _____ Date _____

Summary: People of the South

First Peoples in the South

Native Americans lived in the South for thousands of years before Europeans came in the 1500s. They planted crops and became skilled farmers. Europeans later grew rice and tobacco. They used the South's rich soil and warm weather. Tobacco became an important export. In 1619, the first enslaved Africans were brought to the colony of Jamestown. They were forced to work for free in the colony.

A Plantation Economy

Some Europeans started huge farms called plantations. Most plantations only grew one crop. The main crops were rice, tobacco, cotton, hemp, indigo, and sugar. Inventions helped planters reduce costs and make bigger profits.

Plantations were like small villages. The owners lived in big houses. They had fine clothing, jewels, and art. Enslaved Africans lived in rough cabins and had few belongings. Most southerners did not enslave people.

Northern states passed laws that made slavery illegal. Many southerners said their economy depended on slavery. In 1861, eleven southern states left the United States to start their own country. A Civil War between the North and South began. After four years, the South lost. Slavery was outlawed. More than 4 million African Americans were freed.

Civil Rights and Progress

One hundred years after the Civil War, African Americans still struggled for their civil rights. Slavery had ended, but they did not have equal treatment. Many Americans worked to win equality for all people.

In 1954, separate schools for white and black children were outlawed. Martin Luther King Jr. helped organize a bus boycott after Rosa Parks refused to give up her seat to a white person. The bus company finally agreed to treat all riders equally.

Other groups, including women, American Indians, and Latinos began to demand their civil rights. Women won the right to vote in 1920. Today, people from different backgrounds hold important positions in all areas of American life.

Before You Read
Find and underline each vocabulary word.

export *noun*, a product that is sent out of the country to be sold or traded

boycott *noun*, a protest in which people refuse to do business with a person or company

civil rights *noun*, the rights that every citizen has by law

After You Read

REVIEW **Why did farmers in the South grow tobacco and rice?** Highlight words that tell about the land and climate.

REVIEW **In what ways were the lives of plantation owners and enslaved workers different?** Circle the paragraph that tells about plantation life.

REVIEW **Why did African Americans boycott and protest in the 1950s and 1960s?** Highlight words that tell what people wanted.

Name _____ Date _____

Summary: Resources and Economy

Production in the South

Southerners use natural resources to produce goods and services. They use water moving through dams to make electricity. Farmers grow food. People mine coal and pump oil from underground. They catch ocean fish.

Producers turn these raw materials into many different products. The products are sold to consumers. Producers can also be consumers. They often have to buy supplies before they can make their product. For instance, owners of textile mills buy raw cotton. They spin the cotton to produce cotton yarn. Other manufacturers buy the cotton yarn to make T-shirts.

A Diverse Economy

In the past, farming was the most important part of the South's economy. It is still important. Texas, North Carolina, and Georgia rank in the top ten in numbers of U.S. farm jobs. Farmers produce rice, cotton, tobacco, sugar cane, oranges, hogs, chickens, and cattle. Other Southerners work in cotton mills and textile factories. They make yarn, cloth, and carpets. In Georgia, Arkansas, and Alabama people use trees to produce lumber and paper. People in West Virginia, Kentucky, and Texas mine coal. The coal is used to create energy. Many Southerners work in ground and air transportation. Others work in the tourism, aerospace, and oil industries. The federal government is one of the biggest employers in the South.

The economy is controlled by choices businesses and consumers make. Businesses choose which products to make. They choose how much money to charge for their products. Consumers choose which products to buy. Sometimes things happen that affect those choices. Imagine a frost hurt an orange grove in Florida. The price of orange juice would go up because of scarcity. Consumers have to decide if they are willing to pay more for this product. What someone gives up to get something else is called the opportunity cost. Every economic choice has an opportunity cost.

Before You Read
Find and underline each vocabulary word.

dam *noun*, a barrier built across a waterway to control the flow and level of water

producer *noun*, someone who makes or sells goods or services

consumer *noun*, someone who buys goods and services

scarcity *noun*, when there are not enough resources to provide a product or service that people want

opportunity cost *noun*, what someone gives up to get something else

After You Read

REVIEW **What factors of production are needed to create cotton T-shirts?** Highlight sentences that tell how a T-shirt is made.

REVIEW **What choices do producers and consumers make?** Underline sentences that tell about choices.

Answers continued

Summary: What's Special About the Upper South

Before You Read

Find and underline each vocabulary word.

transportation *noun*, the business of carrying people or goods from one place to another

hub *noun*, a major center of activity

research *verb*, to study something carefully to learn more about it

communication *noun*, the exchange of information

Where People Live

The Upper South has six states: Kentucky, Tennessee, Virginia, Arkansas, North Carolina, and West Virginia. Much of the land is rural and forested, but most of the people live in cities and towns. Farmers grow and sell cotton, tobacco, and rice. They raise chickens, cattle, and horses.

Cities in the Upper South are important places for business. Memphis is a busy transportation center and distribution hub. Big highways, train lines, and the Mississippi River pass through Memphis. Many people in Memphis work to distribute goods throughout the area. The health care and tourism industries are also very important.

After You Read

REVIEW What makes Memphis an important business center? Draw a box around the paragraph that tells why Memphis is special.

Tourists enjoy outdoor activities. They can hunt for diamonds in an Arkansas diamond mine. Music lovers go to Nashville to hear country music. History lovers visit the homes of George Washington and Thomas Jefferson. They can also visit Colonial Williamsburg.

Working in the Upper South

Many companies have moved to the Upper South. They like the region because of its mild climate and educated workers. Many people work in transportation, farming, and tourism. Manufacturing, especially textiles, is an important industry in the Upper South. More than half the furniture sold in the United States is made in High Point, North Carolina. Mining makes West Virginia a leading producer of coal.

REVIEW Describe two of the major industries of the Upper South. Circle words that name industries.

The biggest research center in the United States, Research Triangle Park, is in North Carolina. About 45,000 people work there. They explore new ideas in medicine, computers, and communications. New forms of communication use technology to send messages quickly over long distances. They include cell phones, e-mail, and the Internet.

Summary: What's Special About the Lower South

Before You Read

Find and underline each vocabulary word.

ethnic group *noun*, people who share the same culture, including language, music, food, and art

planned community *noun*, a place to live that is mapped out ahead of time

pollution *noun*, anything that makes the land, water, or air impure or dirty

Where People Live

There are eight states in the Lower South: Texas, Oklahoma, Louisiana, Mississippi, Alabama, Florida, Georgia, and South Carolina. The climate of the Lower South is mostly warm and damp. Texas and Oklahoma are mostly dry. Many ethnic groups live in the region. Many Cuban Americans, Puerto Ricans, Seminole Indians, and African Americans live in Florida. Cajuns and Creoles live in Louisiana.

Houston is the largest city in the South. Oil was found near Houston in 1901. The Houston Ship Channel was built in 1914. It connected Houston to Galveston Bay on the Gulf of Mexico. Today, Houston is one of the three biggest U.S. ports. The world's biggest medical center is also in Houston. The NASA/Johnson Space Center is nearby. Many people in Houston live in planned communities. There are also rural areas in the Lower South. The only state in the Lower South without a coastline is Oklahoma. Many people catch and sell seafood, especially shrimp. In Mississippi, people raise and sell catfish. Texas has big cattle ranches. People in Florida grow oranges and other fruits.

After You Read

REVIEW How did natural resources affect the growth of Houston? Underline the sentence that tells you what happened in 1901.

Work and Recreation

The mild climate makes tourism an important industry in the Lower South. Tourists enjoy hiking, rafting, and fishing. They go to Florida's theme parks. The Mississippi Delta region is the birthplace of a type of music called the blues. New Orleans is the home of jazz. Cajun and zydeco music are popular in Louisiana. Thousands of people work in the four space research centers located in the Lower South. Scientists in Louisiana research pollution.

REVIEW What are two kinds of work people do in the Lower South? Highlight sentences that tell about work people do.

Answers

Name _____ Date _____

Summary: Land and Climate

Land and Water of the Midwest

The Midwest lies in the middle of the country. Canada lies to the north. The Midwest is mostly flat, with some hilly areas. The Great Lakes are in the eastern part of this region. This area has deep forests. In the north, pine forests can survive the cold winters. The Great Plains lie to the west of the Great Lakes. In these states, the climate is drier. Prairie grasses cover much of the land. Farmers turned prairies into farmland. They grow corn and wheat.

The five Great Lakes are the world's largest body of fresh water. Glaciers created these five lakes. Rivers and canals connect them to the Atlantic Ocean and the Gulf of Mexico. Ships can reach the lakes through these waterways.

The Mississippi River is another great waterway. With its tributaries, the Missouri and Ohio rivers, it is part of the largest river system in the country. Dams and levees help stop flooding. Locks on waterways help ships pass waterfalls. Before railroads, travel on waterways was faster and less expensive than traveling on land.

Climate, Plants, Animals

The Midwest can have severe weather. It has no ocean nearby to warm the land in winter and cool it in the summer. The Great Lakes are not as big as an ocean, but they affect the climate. They add moisture to the air.

Winters are cold, and there are big snowstorms called blizzards. People wear layers of clothes and use covered walkways. They go skiing, skating, and ice fishing. In the summer, there are tornadoes with strong, whirling winds. Plants and animals also adapt to the climate. Prairie grass has deep roots to find water. Some birds migrate to warmer places in the winter. Prairie dogs live underground. Buffalo once lived on the Great Plains. They had thick fur. Hunters killed most of them for their skins. Then people started protecting buffalo. Now there are about 150,000 buffalo in the United States.

Before You Read
Find and underline each vocabulary word.

prairie *noun*, dry, mostly flat grassland with few trees

tributary *noun*, a river or stream that flows into another river

levee *noun*, a high river bank that stops the river from overflowing

lock *noun*, part of a waterway that is closed off by gates

After You Read

REVIEW **What are the major regions and waterways of the Midwest?** Circle the words that name a region or waterway of the Midwest.

REVIEW **How have people and wildlife adapted to the climate of the Midwest?** Underline sentences tell what people, animals and plants do to survive in cold winters and hot summers.

Name _____ Date _____

Summary: Resources and Economy

Using Midwestern Resources

The Midwest has many natural resources. Water, rich soil, and minerals helped the region become a major farming and manufacturing center. Water is an important resource. Farmers water crops with it. Rivers and lakes provide transportation.

Large manufacturing cities have grown along waterways. The rich soil and climate support forests that provide lumber and other wood products. The Midwest produces corn, wheat, and soybeans. Farmers also grow hay, fruits, and vegetables. They raise hogs and dairy cows. Some workers make food products, such as jam or cereal. Others build tractors. Miners dig minerals from the ground. Lead is used to make batteries and computers. Iron ore is used to make steel. Steel is used to make cars, boats, planes, and bridges.

The Midwest's Economy

Many manufacturers build factories in the Midwest. The region has many natural resources. It has skilled workers. It has waterways for moving goods. Service industries also have grown in the transportation industry provide a service. They move raw materials to factories and finished products to stores. Indianapolis, Chicago, and Kansas City are important transportation hubs. Banking, health services, and communications are also important service industries.

The concepts of supply and demand can help you understand the economy. The supply is how much of a product producers make. The demand is how much of that product consumers will buy at different prices. If there is a big demand for a product and a small supply, the producer may raise the price of the product.

For example, a company makes a new cereal. If many people want to buy it, the price rises. People pay more for it. But if the price is too high, people may stop buying. The demand for the product falls. If demand stays high, the company will make more. As the supply rises, the price drops. The government helps farmers when supply and demand vary by keeping farm prices from dropping too low.

Before You Read
Find and underline each vocabulary word.

supply *noun*, how much of a product producers will make at different prices

demand *noun*, how much of a product consumers will buy at different prices

After You Read

REVIEW **Name two midwestern industries.** Circle two words that tell what the Midwest is a center for.

REVIEW **Why have certain businesses grown in the Midwest?** There are three reasons why businesses grew in the Midwest. Draw a box around the sentences that name the reasons.

Answers continued

Name _____ Date _____

Summary: The Great Lakes States

Before You Read
Find and underline each vocabulary word.

elevated train *noun,* a railway that runs above the ground on raised tracks

wages *noun,* the payments for work

Where People Live

The Great Lakes states are Ohio, Indiana, Illinois, Michigan, Wisconsin, and Minnesota. Each state borders a Great Lake. The northern states, Michigan, Wisconsin, and Minnesota, have thick forests. The southern Great Lakes states have good farmland. Most people live in cities or in suburbs near cities.

Chicago is the biggest city in the region. It is an important center for business, manufacturing, and transportation because of its location near waterways. As Chicago grew, the city built public transportation. The elevated train carries many people without getting in the way of busy city traffic.

The Great Lakes states also have more than 400,000 farms. In recent years, farmers started using more machines and fewer workers to grow crops. People in rural areas usually earn less money, but they also pay less for living than city people.

Tourists visit the Great Lakes states to camp, fish, boat, or swim. Winter activities like snowmobiling and ice fishing are popular. In cities, people like to visit sports arenas and museums.

After You Read

REVIEW What is an advantage of the elevated train? Circle the words that tell why the train works well in Chicago.

REVIEW How can the growth of suburbs affect the environment? Underline two sentences that tell why suburbs can cause environmental problems.

Leaving Cities

People once moved to cities looking for better jobs and lives than they had in rural areas. Now many people live in the suburbs and travel to cities to work and shop. Some businesses have moved to the suburbs. Some people can work at home using new technology. Cities have problems when people leave. Buildings and homes may be empty, and crime rises. Fast-growing suburbs can also cause environmental problems. Building may not leave enough natural areas for people to enjoy. Air pollution increases because many people drive instead of walking. Cities like Detroit are rebuilding their downtowns to get people to live there again. Cities also work to improve public transportation and protect open space. This may improve life in some cities.

Name _____ Date _____

Summary: People of the Midwest

Before You Read
Find and underline each vocabulary word.

homestead *noun,* a piece of land given to someone to settle and farm there

reservation *noun,* land set aside by the government for American Indians

assembly line *noun,* a way of manufacturing goods where each worker does one small part of the job

The Midwest's First People

American Indians have lived in the Midwest for centuries. Each Indian nation has its own culture. Woodland Indians farmed and built houses with wood frames. Plains Indians followed and hunted the buffalo herds on the Great Plains. Spanish explorers brought the first horses to North America. Soon Plains Indians were using horses to hunt and travel.

Indians traded furs with Europeans for metal tools. Europeans took land to settle. England and France went to war for control of the Ohio Valley. Pontiac, leader of the Ottawa, fought against the English. In 1763 the British defeated the French. The Ottawa were defeated two years later. About 4,700 Ottawa still live in the area.

After You Read

REVIEW How did horses change the lives of the Plains Indians long ago? Circle the sentence that tells you the answer.

REVIEW What were two reasons that the United States grew? Highlight the sentences that tell how the United States got more land.

REVIEW Why did midwestern cities grow? Underline the sentence that tells you the answer.

Early Settlers

The United States took control of the Northwest Territory in 1783. In 1803, Thomas Jefferson bought the Louisiana Territory from France. Jefferson sent Lewis and Clark to explore the region.

Congress passed the Homestead Act of 1862. It gave land to anyone who would settle and stay for five years. Settlers and immigrants from the east came to farm. The government gave land to soldiers. Life was often hard. There were not enough trees to build wooden houses. People built houses of sod. The Indians were pushed from their land. Most were forced to live on reservations.

Midwestern Cities

Midwestern cities grew because of industry and transportation routes. In the late 1800s, many people moved from farms to cities to find factory jobs. Factories used the assembly line to make goods cheaply and quickly.

After World War I, many African Americans moved to the Midwest to get factory work. St. Louis and Minneapolis grew because they were close to natural resources and the Mississippi River. The river provided power for mills. These cities became manufacturing and food processing centers.

Answers

Name _____ Date _____

Summary: Land and Climate

Before You Read
Find and underline each vocabulary word.
geothermal *adjective*, heat from beneath the Earth's crust
irrigation *noun*, a way of supplying land with water
hydroelectric power *noun*, electricity produced from flowing water
arid *adjective*, very dry

After You Read
REVIEW **What are three major landforms found in the West?** Circle words that name landforms. Draw a box around the names of specific landforms.

REVIEW **What factors influence temperature in the West?** Underline the sentence that tells you the answer.

Land and Water of the West

The West is divided into the Southwest, Mountain, and Pacific States. Most western states are east of the Pacific Ocean between Mexico and Canada. Alaska and Hawaii are separated from the other states by land and water. The West has many different landforms and climate regions. There are (mountain ranges) and (valleys, deserts) and (rain forests, glaciers and volcanoes.)

The [Rocky Mountains] formed as tectonic plates pushed against each other. This caused the earth's crust to fold. The [Cascade Mountains] formed when melted lava from a volcano bubbled up through openings in the earth's crust. This released geothermal energy. Between the mountain ranges there are valleys, (basins) and flat, raised areas called plateaus. Glaciers carved valleys such as [Yosemite Valley.] Rivers wore away the rock and made deep (canyons) like the [Grand Canyon.]

Water, Climate, and Wildlife

Many rivers flow west from the Rockies. The water is used for irrigation. Most people live on the coast because the land is so dry. Dams are used to produce hydroelectric power. Temperatures in the West are affected by the Pacific Ocean, elevation, and latitude. Cool, moist air flows east from the Pacific Ocean. This gives the northern coast mild temperatures and more rain than the south. As moist air goes over the mountains, it drops rain and snow on the western side. This air is dry as it goes down the eastern side. This makes the climate arid. Places at high elevations are colder. Alaska is in the northern latitudes, so it has short summers and long winters.

Plants and animals depend on climate. Tropical plants grow in Hawaii. Cactuses grow in arid areas. Sequoias and redwoods grow in wet coastal areas. Bristlecone pines live in the mountains. Elk, bighorn sheep, and cougars live there too. Lizards, scorpions, and snakes live in the hot dry Southwest. In Alaska there are moose, bears, and condors.

Name _____ Date _____

Summary: The Plains States

Before You Read
Find and underline each vocabulary word.
population density *noun*, a measure of how many people live in an area
grain elevator *noun*, a building used to store wheat or other grains

After You Read
REVIEW **Where are most major cities of the Plains States located?** Highlight the sentence that explains why cities formed near rivers.

REVIEW **In what ways do people use the rural areas of the Plains States?** Underline a sentence that tells how farmers use the land. Circle three popular activities people enjoy.

Where People Live

The Plains States are North Dakota, South Dakota, Nebraska, Kansas, Iowa, and Missouri. Iowa and Missouri are in the Central Lowlands, a region with deep fertile soil. The other Plains States are higher, drier, and rockier. They have sandhills and badlands. Wind and water made unusual shapes in the land.

Most major cities formed near rivers. In the past it was easier for people to travel on waterways than across land. Most people in the Plains States live in cities, but most of the land is rural. Rural areas have a low population density. For example, in a city, 5,000 people might live in a square mile. In a rural area, only one person might live in an area twice that size. Small towns have fewer people. They also have fewer services and businesses, such as stores or restaurants. Some rural communities have big fairs where farmers show their best animals. People enjoy (horseback riding, fishing, and hunting.)

Rural Lands on the Plains

Much of the Plains States was once a huge prairie. Farmers made farmland by plowing most of the prairie that covered the Great Plains. They use the land for growing crops and raising cattle for beef. Water towers and grain elevators may be the only tall buildings between one town and the next. Tourists visit the area to see Mount Rushmore, a huge sculpture of American presidents, and natural wonders such as Chimney Rock in Nebraska.

American Indians followed buffalo herds on the Great Plains for centuries. As the United States grew, the U.S. army fought the Indians and took their land. The United States broke many promises it made with the Indian nations. The U.S. government created reservations. Indians were forced to live on reservations. The Lakota nation, also called the Sioux, has two large reservations in South Dakota.

Answers continued

CHAPTER 9, LESSON 3

Name _____ Date _____

Summary: The People of the West

Early Peoples of the West

Many scientists think people first came to the West over 15,000 years ago. The Aleut and Inuit lived in the North. The Hopi and Navajo lived in the Southwest. They learned to use the resources where they lived. Those near the sea fished. Others hunted and farmed.

About 700 years ago, people we now call the Pueblo people lived near the Rio Grande. They irrigated land to grow crops. They gathered wild plants and hunted animals. They made baskets and pottery and traded them for salt, food, and animal hides. On the northwest coast, the Tlingit people gathered wild plants, hunted, and fished. They traded seal oil for furs and made blankets that showed stories. Pueblo, Tlingit, and other American Indian groups still live in the West.

Spanish Settlements

The Spanish conquered Mexico in 1519 and called it New Spain. Then they went north to look for gold. The Spanish took the Indians' land. The Spanish wanted Indians to give up their culture and become Christians, so they started missions.

In 1821, Mexico won independence from Spain. Texas split off from Mexico in 1836 and joined the United States in 1845. Mexico and the United States went to war the following year. The United States won. Mexico had to give the Southwest to the United States. Spanish and Mexican influence is still strong there. Many people speak Spanish. Many foods and festivals in the region come from Spain or Mexico.

More People Go West

Gold was found in California in 1848. Many people moved west in wagon trains hoping to get rich or buy cheap land. They took American Indian land. American Indians were forced to move to separate places called reservations. After Chinese immigrants helped build the transcontinental railroad in 1869, the West grew fast. In 1959, Hawaii and Alaska were the last two states to join the Union. Now there are 50 states.

Before You Read

Find and underline each vocabulary word.

mission *noun,* a settlement for teaching religion to local people

wagon train *noun,* a line of wagons that carried settlers and their belongings

transcontinental railroad *noun,* train system that linked the East and the West

After You Read

REVIEW What did different groups who settled the West have in common? Underline a sentence that tells what the Aleut, Inuit, Hopi, and Navajo learned to use in the West.

REVIEW Why did the Spanish build missions in New Spain? Draw a box around the words that tell the answer.

REVIEW How did the transcontinental railroad affect population in the West? Circle the words that tell what happened to the population after the transcontinental railroad was built.

CHAPTER 9, LESSON 2

Name _____ Date _____

Summary: Resources and Economy

Using Resources

People in the West use their natural resources to make goods and sell services. Soil and climate are important resources. Farmers grow fruit and vegetables to sell. Many people have jobs processing and shipping food. Trees are also a key resource. People cut trees down and make them into lumber and paper at mills. People catch fish in the ocean.

The West's climate helps many businesses. People make movies and tourists come for vacations. Aircraft companies build airplanes. People mine natural mineral resources, such as copper, gold, uranium, and coal. Other people make products from the minerals. The U.S. government owns a lot of land in the West. Some of it is in national parks, such as Glacier, Yellowstone, and Grand Canyon.

The West's Economy

Many businesses in the West do research or provide services. Many companies in the West make computer products, software, or aircraft. Technology is important to the economy, especially in the Southwest and Pacific States. Many businesses have a specialization. For example, a company might make just one part of a computer, not the whole computer. The company can improve how that part works and also learn to make it at a lower cost.

Some people are skilled workers. They have special training or education. For example, many people in the computer industry have advanced training. They research and invent computer products. For some jobs, workers need no special training. Businesses can hire unskilled workers. Skilled workers usually make more money than unskilled workers.

Many people in Hawaii and Alaska work for the government. In all regions of the West many people work in service jobs, like health care or construction.

Before You Read

Find and underline each vocabulary word.

national park *noun,* an area of land set aside by the federal government

specialization *noun,* when a business makes only a few goods or provides just one service

skilled worker *noun,* someone who has special training or education to do a job

unskilled worker *noun,* someone who does not need special training or education to do a job

After You Read

REVIEW What are two ways that people use resources in the West? Underline two sentences that tell what resources people in the West grow or use.

REVIEW Which parts of the West have the most technology companies? Draw a box around the sentence that tells where technology is important to the economy.

Answers

Name _____ Date _____

Summary: The Southwest

Where People Live

The four Southwest states are Utah, Nevada, New Mexico, and Arizona. The climate is dry. They have mountains, plateaus, deserts, and other landforms.

Big cities grew in the deserts. Phoenix is the largest city in the Southwest. The first people to live there were the Hohokam. They built irrigation canals to water their crops. Later, European settlers found the canals and rebuilt the settlement. They built dams on rivers to provide water. Today, Phoenix has a steady supply of water. Over one million people live there. Buildings in Phoenix are made in Spanish, Mexican, and American Indian styles.

Thousands of American Indians live in the Southwest in cities and on pueblos. The Navajo Indian reservation is the largest in the nation. It covers 16 million acres in Arizona, New Mexico, and Utah. The Pueblo, Hopi, Zuni, Acoma, and Laguna Indians live in pueblos near the Rio Grande. Some of the oldest ranches in North America are in the Southwest. People raise sheep, cattle, and horses on these ranches.

The Southwest Today

Millions of tourists come to the Southwest each year. They want to see the high mountains, wild rivers, and beautiful canyons. Weathering and erosion carved the Grand Canyon and many natural arches in Utah. There are ghost towns and national parks to visit. People ride bicycles and hike. They paddle the rivers and swim in lakes. They can enjoy Mexican food, Indian festivals, and rodeos. People in the Southwest speak English, Spanish, and Indian languages.

Water is scarce in this region. Reservoirs are made to store water. People practice water conservation. Plants that don't need extra watering are used in parks and public places. Farmers conserve water by using drip irrigation. Drip irrigation does not flood the fields with water. It allows water to slowly soak into the soil.

Before You Read

Find and underline each vocabulary word.

weathering *noun,* the breakdown of rock caused by wind, water, and weather

conservation *noun,* using something carefully and not wasting it

After You Read

REVIEW Describe how the Spanish, Mexicans, and American Indians have influenced life in the Southwest. Who were the first people to live in Phoenix? How did they get water? Which American Indian groups live in the Southwest today? Buildings in Phoenix are made in different styles. What are they? Circle the words and sentences that tell you the answers.

REVIEW How do people conserve water? What kinds of plants are used in parks and public places? How do farmers conserve water? Underline the sentences that tell you the answers.

Right sheet:

Name _____ Date _____

Summary: What's Special About the Mountain States

Cities and Rural Areas

The Rocky Mountains run through Colorado, Idaho, Montana, and Wyoming. These states are called the Mountain States. There are also hills, plateaus, plains, and valleys. The Sioux, Cheyenne, Arapaho, Apache, Ute, and Crow Indians were the first people to live in the region.

Denver is the capital of Colorado. It is on a mile-high plain east of the Rockies. The mountains block moisture coming from the west. This keeps the climate dry.

Most people in the Mountain States live in the cities. The cities are centers for entertainment, education, and health care. Some people live in rural areas. Here, the land is rugged. The winters are long and cold. People raise cattle and sheep. There are usually only a few doctors, dentists, schools, and other services in these areas. People living in rural areas travel to cities to get supplies and services.

Recreation and Tourism

Many people work in mining, farming, and forestry industries in the Mountain States. Tourism is also an important industry. The high elevation of the Mountain States creates a perfect place for winter sports. Tourists come to ski in the winter. They camp, hike, fish, and ride horses in the summer. Tourists spend money and buy services, such as hotels and meals. Tourism creates jobs.

There are many national parks in the region, including Yellowstone and Glacier. National parks protect wilderness areas and historical places. Yellowstone is the nation's oldest national park. It is a complete ecosystem with many different habitats. Animals like the buffalo were almost extinct. Now they are protected in the park. Yellowstone is also famous for its geysers. The heat inside the earth causes geysers to shoot out hot water. Visitors can also see hot springs and bubbling mud pots.

Before You Read

Find and underline each vocabulary word.

ecosystem *noun,* an environment and all its living things, working together as a unit

habitat *noun,* the natural home of a plant or animal

extinct *adjective,* no longer existing

After You Read

REVIEW Name two things the four Mountain States have in common. Circle the landforms that the Mountain States share. Highlight a sentence that tells where most people live.

REVIEW What attracts visitors to the Mountain States? What do tourists do in the summer and the winter? Which national parks can they visit? Underline the sentences that tell the answers.

Answers *continued*

Name _____ Date _____

Summary: What's Special About the Pacific States

CHAPTER 10, LESSON 3

Before You Read
Find and underline each vocabulary word.

seasonal *adjective,* happening at certain times of the year

migrant worker *noun,* a worker who moves from place to place to find seasonal work

After You Read

REVIEW What is the importance of the seaports on the Pacific coast? Underline the sentence that tells what happens at port cities.

REVIEW What industries support farming in the Pacific States? Draw a box around two sentences that tell how farm crops are turned into food products.

Cities of the Pacific States

The Pacific States are Alaska, California, Oregon, Washington, and Hawaii. Four states are on the coast of the Pacific Ocean. The fifth, Hawaii, is a group of islands in the middle of the Pacific. The ocean affects the climate of all these states.

Seattle is Washington State's biggest city. It is a center for business and industry. Many people there work in technology industries. Other big cities in the Pacific States are port cities, such as Portland, Oregon, Los Angeles, California, and Honolulu, Hawaii. Ships from these ports carry goods all over the world. San Francisco, California, is an international banking center. Los Angeles is home to the movie and television industry.

Agricultural Activities

The different climates of the Pacific States let farmers grow many crops. It is cool and wet in the northwest coastal regions. Farmers grow peas, pears, broccoli, apples, and strawberries.

East of the Cascade Mountains, farmers grow wheat and sugar beets. In southern California, where the growing season is very long, farmers can grow citrus fruits, almonds, kiwi, and figs. In tropical Hawaii, they grow 650,000 tons of pineapple a year.

Harvesting, or picking the crops, is seasonal work. Each crop is picked at a certain time of year. Farmers need migrant workers to do this work. Many migrant workers live in bad conditions and are paid very little.

The cities on the coast support farming in rural areas. Cities have factories where farm crops are turned into food products. Workers in factories can fruits and vegetables, make juices, and bake goods.

Tourists in the Pacific States enjoy skiing, surfing, and visiting national parks. They can see Arctic wilderness in Alaska, active volcanoes in Hawaii, and glaciers and a rainforest in Washington State.

Resources for Reaching All Learners
Copyright © Houghton Mifflin Company. All rights reserved.

27

Use with *States and Regions*, pp. 288–291

Name _____ Date _____

Summary: United States Government

CHAPTER 11, LESSON 1

Before You Read
Find and underline each vocabulary word.

citizen *noun,* a person born in a country or who promises to be loyal to the country

democracy *noun,* a system in which the people hold the power of government

representative *noun,* a person who acts for a group of people

election *noun,* the way voters choose people to serve in government

constitution *noun,* a plan for setting up and running a government

After You Read

REVIEW What is the job of representatives in our democratic system? Underline the words that tell what representatives do for the people who elect them.

REVIEW Why are there three branches of government? The Constitution set up three branches of government. Why? Draw a box around the sentence that tells the answer.

Government by the People

One role of our government is to protect our rights. The United States government is "by the people." This means that the people create the government and decide who will lead them. Our government is "of the people." This means that each citizen has a say in the government. Our government is "for the people" because it is for the good of everyone.

The United States is a democracy. The people decide who will lead and what the government will do. But there are too many people to vote on every decision. So people choose representatives, who vote in the government. Representatives make decisions and represent the people. Citizens vote for representatives in an election.

Before 1776, the states were colonies ruled by Great Britain. People in the colonies wanted to be free from British rule. They wrote the Declaration of Independence to explain why they wanted to break ties with Britain.

The Constitution

The leaders of the United States wrote the Constitution in 1787. The Bill of Rights is part of the Constitution. It protects our rights and freedoms. It makes sure all citizens have freedom, equality, and justice. The Bill of Rights also limits the powers of the government.

The Constitution set up three branches of government. This helps make sure that one branch does not get too powerful. The legislative branch makes laws. Citizens elect representatives to Congress. Congress has two parts, the House of Representatives and the Senate. The executive branch carries out the laws. The President is head of the executive branch. The judicial branch includes questions about the laws. This branch includes the courts. The Supreme Court is the highest court in the United States. It has the final say on laws. The Supreme Court decides what laws mean and if they are allowed by the Constitution.

Resources for Reaching All Learners
Copyright © Houghton Mifflin Company. All rights reserved.

28

Use with *States and Regions*, pp. 308–311

Resources for Reaching All Learners
Copyright © Houghton Mifflin Company. All rights reserved.

94

Use with *States and Regions*

Answers

Summary: North American Neighbors

Our Northern Neighbor: Canada

The United States is part of North America. Canada is also in North America. It is north of the United States. Canada is the second largest country in the world in land area. But the United States has nine times more people. The United States trades with Canada more than any other country.

Canada stretches far north into the Arctic Circle, so the climate is cold. Mountain ranges on the coast block warm winds from the Pacific Ocean. Most people live where it is warmer, on the coasts or on the southern border.

The United States and Canada share landforms, such as the Rocky Mountains and the Great Plains. Forestry is a major industry in Canada.

American Indians have lived in Canada for thousands of years. Settlers from France and Britain came in the 1600s. In Quebec, many people speak French. In other parts of Canada people mostly speak English. Canada has ten provinces and three territories.

Mexico and the Caribbean

Mexico is on the southern border of the United States. It is large and has many regions. The capital, Mexico City, is on the Mexican Plateau. It is one of the world's biggest cities. Mountain ranges go down both coasts. It can be cold in the mountains, but the climate of Mexico is mostly tropical, warm, and dry. The United States trades a lot with Mexico and the Caribbean islands.

The Caribbean islands are southeast of the United States. American Indians lived in the Caribbean and Mexico for thousands of years. In the 1400s, European countries took land for colonies. Spain conquered the Aztec people of Mexico. Spain and other European nations also colonized Caribbean islands. Europeans brought enslaved Africans to the area. Today, most Mexicans speak Spanish and have Spanish or Indian backgrounds. Many people in the Caribbean have African backgrounds.

Before You Read
Find and underline the vocabulary word.

province noun, a unit of government into which a nation is divided

After You Read
REVIEW **How do Canada's area and population compare to those of the United States?** Underline the sentences that tell about Canada's size and how many people live there compared to the United States.

REVIEW **In what ways is the history of Mexico and the Caribbean like the history of the United States?** Circle the sentence that tells who lived in Mexico and the Caribbean before Europeans arrived. Draw a box around the sentence that tells what the Europeans did when they arrived. Then underline the sentence that tells how Africans came to these places.

Summary: Many Regions, One Nation

Linking Regions

Americans share the same government. We have the same values of liberty, equality, and justice. Our nation is connected by railroads, canals, and airports. We are linked by phones, airplanes, and the Internet.

Each connection between states leads to interdependence. For example, farmers in Maryland can sell their crops to families in New Jersey. People in New Jersey can buy food from farmers in Maryland. The farmers and families both depend on each other. These kinds of links are found across the country. They help to bring us together.

The U.S. government works hard to create these links. The U.S. Postal Service connects people and businesses across the country. It helps people communicate and move goods. The government also helped to build a transportation system across the country. The Interstate Highway system helps transport people and goods around the country.

Good transportation and communication help bring prosperity to Americans. The government runs air-traffic control so that airplanes can travel safely. It sets basic rules for television and radio communications. The government and businesses try to make trade grow. The banking system makes trade easier because everyone knows how to pay for goods and services.

Our Common Culture

Americans come from many different places, but we have a shared heritage. This includes language, food, music, holidays, and beliefs. The cultures of all people who live in the United States are part of our heritage. People in every state celebrate Independence Day with fireworks and Memorial Day with parades. People from all regions help when there is need. After the attacks on September 11, 2001, volunteers came to New York City from all over the country to help.

Before You Read
Find and underline each vocabulary word.

interdependence noun, a relationship in which people depend on each other

prosperity noun, wealth and success

heritage noun, traditions that people have honored for many years

volunteer noun, someone who agrees to provide a service without pay

After You Read
REVIEW **In what ways does the United States Postal Service link different parts of the country?** Underline the sentence that tells what the U.S. postal service does.

REVIEW **In what ways do we show our shared culture?** Draw a box around the sentence that describes how people celebrate holidays all over the country.

Answers *continued*

Name _____ Date _____

Summary: World Regions

Before You Read
Find and underline each vocabulary word.

vegetation *noun*, the kinds of plants that grow in a region

dialect *noun*, a regional form of a language

After You Read

REVIEW **What are two kinds of regions?** Highlight words that name kinds of regions.

REVIEW **How can the features of a region affect the people who live there?** Underline sentences that tell how climate or natural resources affect how people in Southeast Asia live. Underline sentences that tell about houses people build.

Regions of the World

People divide the world into different kinds of regions. A region has some shared features, such as landforms, history, culture, or crops. Hemispheres are regions that include half of the earth. The United States is in the Northern and Western Hemispheres. Continents are another kind of region. The United States is part of the North American continent.

Landform regions can be identified by common landforms. They are based on the shape of the land. Mountain regions may be rugged with steep slopes. Plains regions may have broad, flat land. Continents have many landform regions. Climate regions, such as Arctic zones and tropical zones, are another way people divide the world. Regions can be defined by the amount of rainfall they get or by vegetation. Regions can also be defined by human features, such as a shared economic system, language, or religion.

Regions and People

The features of a region affect the lives of its people. For example, the warm, wet climate of Southeast Asia is good for growing rice. Rice is the most important food there and in most of Asia. Rice plays a role in the religions of Asia. In Bali people think of rice as a great gift and have religious ceremonies to show their respect. People who live in arctic regions cannot farm because it is too cold. Fishing and hunting are central to their lives. Resources of a region also affect how people live. In forested regions, people build their houses of wood. In warmer regions, people build houses of cement to stay cool. There can be differences within regions too. In India there are people who speak different dialects and have different religious beliefs. Different kinds of regions can overlap. A mountain region can include two different language regions. Learning about regions helps us understand the world and the people in it.

Name _____ Date _____

Summary: Central and South America

Before You Read
Find and underline each vocabulary word.

isthmus *noun*, a narrow strip of land that connects two larger land areas

rain forest *noun*, dense forest that gets large amounts of rainfall every year

After You Read

REVIEW **What made Panama a good place to build a canal?** Draw a box around the sentence that tells how wide Panama is.

REVIEW **Name two major physical features of the South American continent.** Circle the names of a major landform and a river in South America.

Central America

Central America has seven countries. They are all part of North America. Central America is long and narrow. The isthmus of Panama, at the southern end, is only about 50 miles wide. The United States took the land in 1903 and built a canal so ships could go from the Atlantic to the Pacific oceans. The Panama Canal opened in 1914.

Mountains run down the middle of Central America. Central America is tropical. There are rain forests with many kinds of plants and animals. American Indians, such as the Maya, have lived there for thousands of years. Then European countries, such as Spain and England, took land for colonies. Today there are people of Spanish, American Indian, and mixed background.

Agriculture is an important industry in Central America. Major crops are bananas, sugar, and coffee. Many people are poor and only grow enough to live.

South America

South America has twelve countries. It is just south of Central America. A major landform is the Andes Mountains. There are high peaks and some volcanoes. The Amazon River flows through the world's largest rain forest. Much of South America is tropical, with a wet, hot climate. But in the mountains, temperatures can be cold. The southern part of the continent almost reaches the frozen continent of Antarctica.

American Indians have lived in South America for thousands of years. In the 1500s, Spain and Portugal took over most of South America. They forced the Indians to work for them and also brought enslaved Africans. Later, immigrants from Europe and Asia came to live in South America.

South America is rich in minerals, oil, and metals. Industry is growing, but most people farm. Other resources are the plants in the forest. South Americans are working hard to protect the rain forest. Industry is growing, but most people live by farming.

Answers

Name _____ Date _____

Summary: Working Together

Before You Read
Find and underline each vocabulary word.

international law *noun*, a set of basic rules to which the United States and many other countries have agreed

nongovernmental organization *noun*, a group that is not part of a national government

After You Read

REVIEW When was the United Nations formed, and for what purposes? Underline the sentence that tells when and why the United Nations was formed.

REVIEW What are some goals of NGOs? Underline words that tell what NGOs do.

Nations Work Together

The United States works with other countries for common goals. After World War II, the United States helped create the United Nations, or UN, to build peace and friendship around the world.

More than 190 countries belong to the UN. Members work together to solve problems. Members wrote the Universal Declaration of Human Rights to protect everyone's basic rights. The World Bank, part of the UN, helps countries build their economies. The World Health Organization works to improve health worldwide. The United States and many other countries have agreed to some basic rules. They are called international law. For example, many countries have agreed on what can and cannot be done in war. Treaties are another example of international law. The UN helps organize trials if crimes were committed in a war.

People Work Together

Nongovernmental organizations (NGOs), such as the International Red Cross or Doctors Without Borders, cross borders between countries to help people. There are thousands of NGOs in the world. They are not part of any country's government. Many work with the UN. They help the poor and sick, give medical care, teach about farming or business, support democracy, and protect human rights. NGOs help when disasters like earthquakes or wars happen.

It is easier for people around the world to communicate now using wireless phones and the Internet. The Internet lets people share information all over the world. People use email and websites to learn new information. Some countries try to control the information their citizens get. New technologies can connect people. This might help bring freedom and change to many.

34

Use with *States and Regions*, pp. 354–357

Name _____ Date _____

Summary: Partners Around the World

Before You Read
Find and underline each vocabulary word.

ally *noun*, a country or group that joins with another country or group for a common purpose

alliance *noun*, an agreement between allies to seek a common goal

treaty *noun*, an official document that defines an agreement between nations

free enterprise *noun*, a system that lets people control their businesses and decide what goods to buy

import *noun*, a product brought in from another country

After You Read

REVIEW Why does the United States form alliances? Highlight the sentences that tell you the answer.

REVIEW Why is international trade important to the United States? Underline the sentence that tells why selling to people in other countries makes trade grow.

United States Allies

The United States has many allies. The United States forms alliances, or agreements, with other countries. Allies help defend each other. The United States also has alliances for trading and sharing scientific research. Alliances are formed by making treaties. The North Atlantic Treaty Organization, NATO, was formed in 1949 between the United States and our European allies. NATO countries agree to defend each other from attack. The North American Free Trade Agreement, or NAFTA, is a trade alliance. It lets Mexico, Canada, and the United States buy and sell goods to each other without paying fees or taxes. The United States also has allies on other continents. Many of our allies believe in a free enterprise system. The United States also trades with countries that do not believe in free enterprise.

Trading Partners

Trade alliances help connect countries through communication and transportation links. These links let goods, services, and information move freely. When businesses sell their goods to people in other countries they can sell more, so trade grows. International trade is the buying and selling of goods between countries. It is an important part of our economy. U.S. businesses sell goods and services worth hundreds of billions of dollars to other countries every year. U.S. consumers also buy hundreds of billions of dollars in imports or goods that come from other countries. Some imported goods cost less than goods made in the United States. People buy cars, clothing, and television sets from other countries. Many people worry that free trade hurts American workers. They think we need laws to protect jobs and the environment. Some countries pass laws to add extra cost to imports. The United States has rules to protect some industries, but also supports free trade. Canada and Mexico are our biggest trading partners. We also trade with China, Japan, South Korea, and nations in Europe. Many European nations formed the European Union trade alliance.

33

Use with *States and Regions*, pp. 348–351

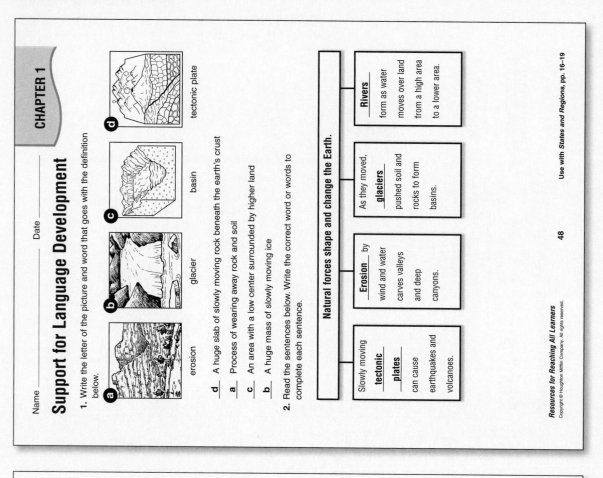

CHAPTER 1

Name _____ Date _____

Support for Language Development

1. Write the letter of the picture and word that goes with the definition below.

erosion (a)   glacier (b)   basin (c)   tectonic plate (d)

d A huge slab of slowly moving rock beneath the earth's crust

a Process of wearing away rock and soil

c An area with a low center surrounded by higher land

b A huge mass of slowly moving ice

2. Read the sentences below. Write the correct word or words to complete each sentence.

Natural forces shape and change the Earth.

Slowly moving **tectonic plates** can cause earthquakes and volcanoes.

Erosion by wind and water carves valleys and deep canyons.

As they moved, **glaciers** pushed soil and rocks to form basins.

Rivers form as water moves over land from a high area to a lower area.

Resources for Reaching All Learners   48   Use with *States and Regions*, pp. 16–19

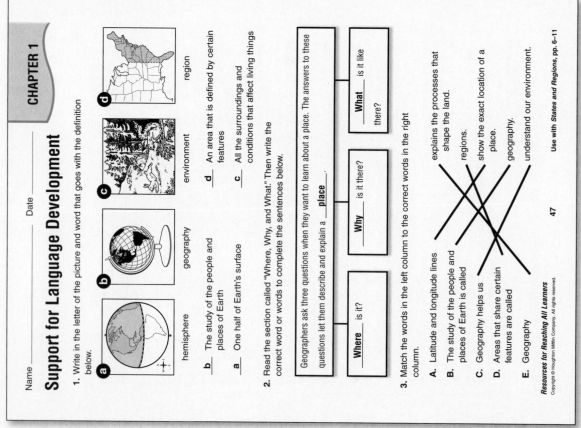

CHAPTER 1

Name _____ Date _____

Support for Language Development

1. Write in the letter of the picture and word that goes with the definition below.

hemisphere (a)   geography (b)   environment (c)   region (d)

b The study of the people and places of Earth

a One half of Earth's surface

d An area that is defined by certain features

c All the surroundings and conditions that affect living things

2. Read the section called "Where, Why, and What." Then write the correct word or words to complete the sentences below.

Geographers ask three questions when they want to learn about a place. The answers to these questions let them describe and explain a **place**.

Where is it?   **Why** is it there?   **What** is it like there?

3. Match the words in the left column to the correct words in the right column.

A. Latitude and longitude lines — show the exact location of a place.

B. The study of the people and places of Earth is called — geography.

C. Geography helps us — understand our environment.

D. Areas that share certain features are called — regions.

E. Geography — explains the processes that shape the land.

Resources for Reaching All Learners   47   Use with *States and Regions*, pp. 6–11

Answers

Name _____ Date _____

Support for Language Development

1. Write the letter of the picture and word that goes with the definition below.

a — government   b — population   c — religion   d — boundary

b the people who live in an area

a a system of making and carrying out rules and laws

d the edge of a region

c a system of faith or worship

2. Read "One Place, Many Regions" on page 39 of your textbook. Look at the Venn diagram. Then fill in the blanks in the sentence below.

The city of Elizabeth is in both the region of ___New York City___ **metropolitan area** and the region of ___New Jersey___.

New York City metropolitan area | Elizabeth | New Jersey

Name _____ Date _____

Support for Language Development

1. Write in the letter of the picture and word that goes with the definition below.

a — product   b — natural resources   c — fossil fuel   d — renewable resources   e — nonrenewable resources

b Things from the natural environment that people use

d Things that the environment can replace after we use them

e Things nature cannot replace after we use them

a Something that is made from natural resources

c An energy source formed by the remains of things that lived long ago

2. Read the section called "Using Resources Wisely." Write the correct word or words to complete each sentence below.

A. You can turn ___off lights___ when you leave a room.

B. You can use ___less water___ when you brush your teeth.

C. You can ___recycle___ the ___bottles___, ___cans___, and ___paper___ you use.

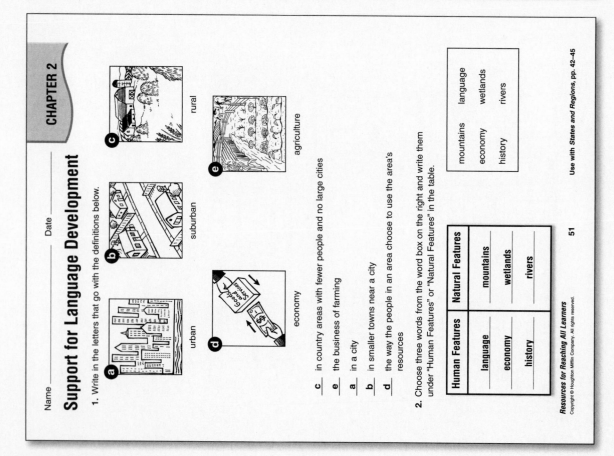

CHAPTER 2

Name _____ Date _____

Support for Language Development

1. Write the letter of the picture and word that goes with the definition below.

precipitation   temperature   climate   elevation

b   the measure of how hot or cold the air is

a   water that falls to the earth as rain, snow, sleet, or hail

d   the height of the land

c   the usual weather conditions in a place over a long period of time

2. Read "Conditions and Climate" on page 53 of your textbook. Then fill in the blanks in the sentences with the correct word or words.

A. The __weather__ describes conditions like wind speed and direction, amount of moisture in the air, and __precipitation__.

B. __Temperature__ is the measure of how hot or cold the air is.

C. __Climate__ is the usual weather conditions over a long period of time.

D. Three factors affect climate: __latitude__, __distance__ from a major body of water, and __elevation__.

Resources for Reaching All Learners
Copyright © Houghton Mifflin Company. All rights reserved.
52
Use with *States and Regions*, pp. 52–57

CHAPTER 2

Name _____ Date _____

Support for Language Development

1. Write in the letters that go with the definitions below.

urban   suburban   rural   economy   agriculture

c   in country areas with fewer people and no large cities

e   the business of farming

a   in a city

b   in smaller towns near a city

d   the way the people in an area choose to use the area's resources

2. Choose three words from the word box on the right and write them under "Human Features" or "Natural Features" in the table.

mountains	language
economy	wetlands
history	rivers

Human Features	Natural Features
language	mountains
economy	wetlands
history	rivers

Resources for Reaching All Learners
Copyright © Houghton Mifflin Company. All rights reserved.
51
Use with *States and Regions*, pp. 42–45

Answers

Name _____ Date _____

Support for Language Development

1. Write the letter of the picture that goes with the definition below.

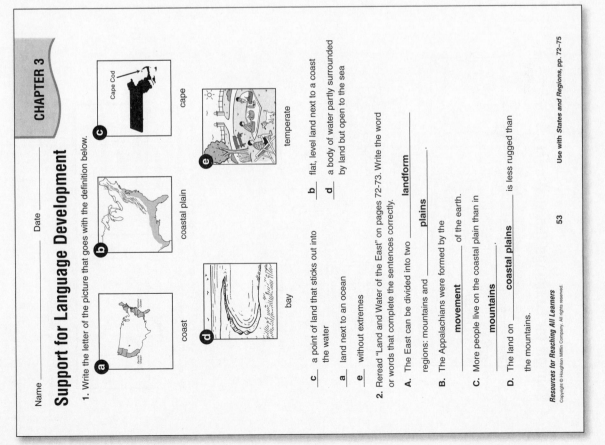

a — market economy
b — profit
c — factors of production
d — human resources
e — capital resources

__e__ the tools, machines, buildings, and other equipment a business uses to make goods or provide services

__c__ the people and materials needed to make goods or provide services

__b__ money left over after a business pays all its expenses

2. Reread "Elements of Business" on page 82 of your textbook. There are 4 factors of production. Write one factor in each oval.

__a__ a system that lets people decide what to make, buy, and sell

__d__ the services, knowledge, skills, and intelligence that workers provide

labor — capital — entrepreneurship — land — **Factors of production**

Name _____ Date _____

Support for Language Development

1. Write the letter of the picture that goes with the definition below.

a — coast
b — coastal plain
c — cape (Cape Cod)
d — bay
e — temperate

__c__ a point of land that sticks out into the water

__a__ land next to an ocean

__e__ without extremes

__b__ flat, level land next to a coast

__d__ a body of water partly surrounded by land but open to the sea

2. Reread "Land and Water of the East" on pages 72-73. Write the word or words that complete the sentences correctly.

A. The East can be divided into two ___landform___ regions: mountains and ___plains___.

B. The Appalachians were formed by the ___movement___ of the earth.

C. More people live on the coastal plain than in ___mountains___.

D. The land on ___coastal plains___ is less rugged than the mountains.

Answers *continued*

Use with *States and Regions*

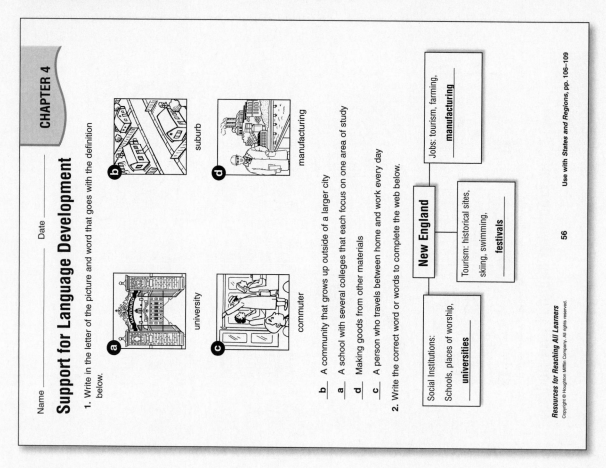

Name _____ Date _____

Support for Language Development

1. Write in the letter of the picture and word that goes with the definition below.

a — university
b — suburb
c — commuter
d — manufacturing

b A community that grows up outside of a larger city

a A school with several colleges that each focus on one area of study

d Making goods from other materials

c A person who travels between home and work every day

2. Write the correct word or words to complete the web below.

New England

Social Institutions:
Schools, places of worship, **universities**

Tourism: historical sites, skiing, swimming, **festivals**

Jobs: tourism, farming, **manufacturing**

Resources for Reaching All Learners
Copyright © Houghton Mifflin Company. All rights reserved.

56   Use with *States and Regions*, pp. 106–109

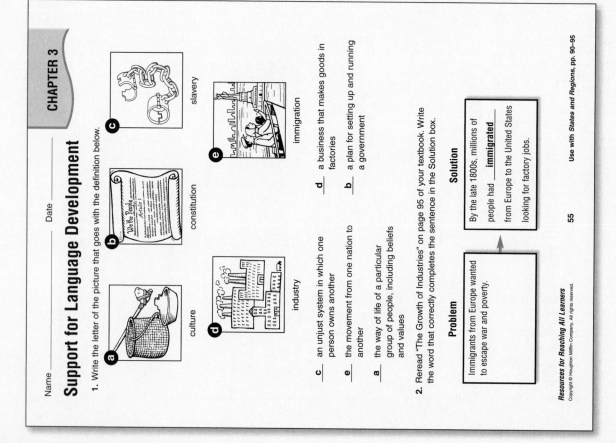

Name _____ Date _____

Support for Language Development

1. Write the letter of the picture that goes with the definition below.

a — culture
b — constitution
c — slavery
d — industry
e — immigration

c an unjust system in which one person owns another

e the movement from one nation to another

a the way of life of a particular group of people, including beliefs and values

d a business that makes goods in factories

b a plan for setting up and running a government

2. Reread "The Growth of Industries" on page 95 of your textbook. Write the word that correctly completes the sentence in the Solution box.

Problem

Immigrants from Europe wanted to escape war and poverty.

Solution

By the late 1800s, millions of people had **immigrated** from Europe to the United States looking for factory jobs.

Resources for Reaching All Learners
Copyright © Houghton Mifflin Company. All rights reserved.

55   Use with *States and Regions*, pp. 90–95

Answers

Name _____ Date _____

Support for Language Development

1. Write the letter of the picture and word that goes with the definition below.

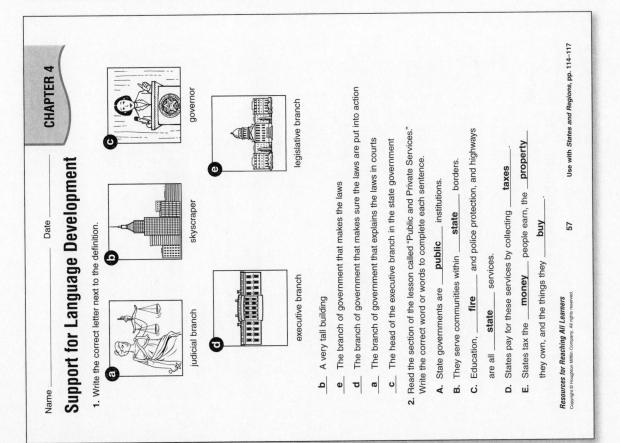

b adapt

d interior

a delta

c peninsula

c A piece of land surrounded by water on three sides

d An area away from the coast or border

a A triangle-shaped area at the mouth of a river

b To change in order to better fit in an environment

2. Read the section of the lesson called "Climate and Wildlife." Then match the areas on the left to the correct descriptions on the right.

A. Ozark highlands — are usually warm

B. coastal areas — winters are mild

C. lowlands — can have severe weather

58   Use with *States and Regions*, pp. 132–135

Name _____ Date _____

Support for Language Development

1. Write the correct letter next to the definition.

c governor

b skyscraper

e legislative branch

a judicial branch

d executive branch

b A very tall building

e The branch of government that makes the laws

d The branch of government that makes sure the laws are put into action

a The branch of government that explains the laws in courts

c The head of the executive branch in the state government

2. Read the section of the lesson called "Public and Private Services." Write the correct word or words to complete each sentence.

A. State governments are   **public**   institutions.

B. They serve communities within   **state**   borders.

C. Education,   **fire**   and police protection, and highways are all   **state**   services.

D. States pay for these services by collecting   **taxes** .

E. States tax the   **money**   people earn, the   **property**   they own, and the things they   **buy** .

57   Use with *States and Regions*, pp. 114–117

Name _____ Date _____

Support for Language Development

1. Write the vocabulary word in the correct space.

export   boycott   civil rights

civil rights — The rights that every citizen has by law

boycott — A protest in which people refuse to do business with a person or company

export — A product that is sent out of the country to be sold or traded

2. Read "The Struggle for Civil Rights." Then read the sentences below. Write the correct word or words to complete each sentence.

Americans worked for equality and **civil** **rights** for all.

1920: Women won the right to **vote**.

1954: African Americans could go to the same **schools** as whites.

1955: The law made **bus** companies treat all passengers **equally**.

Name _____ Date _____

Support for Language Development

1. Write the vocabulary word in the correct space.

opportunity cost   producer   scarcity   consumer   dam

producer

dam

scarcity

consumer

opportunity cost

2. Write the vocabulary word or words that complete each sentence correctly.

A. **Producers** / **dams** use water that runs through to make electricity.

B. **Consumers** buy this electricity.

C. **Scarcity** is when too few products are made for the number of consumers who want to buy them.

D. **Opportunity cost** is when you give up one thing in order to buy another.

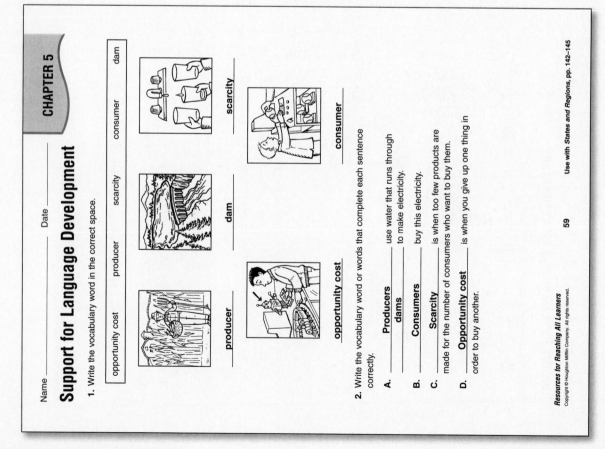

Answers

Support for Language Development

Name _____ Date _____

1. Write the letter of the word that goes with the definition below.

   a ethnic group   **b** planned community   **c** pollution

   c Anything that makes the land, water, or air impure or dirty

   b A place to live that is mapped out ahead of time

   a People who share the same culture, including language, music, food, and art

2. Read the section called "Rural Life." Then write the word or words that complete each sentence correctly.

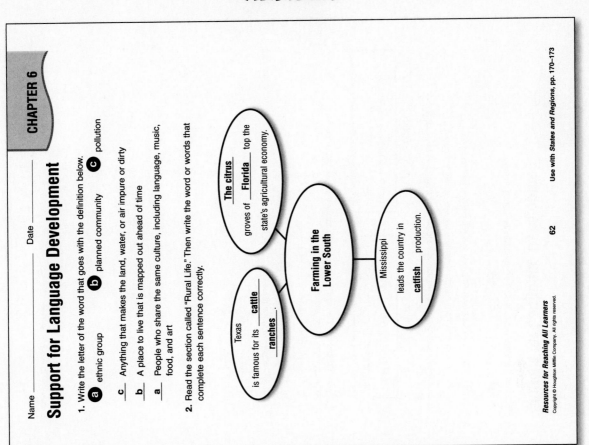

The citrus groves of **Florida** top the state's agricultural economy.

Texas is famous for its **cattle ranches**.

Farming in the Lower South

Mississippi leads the country in **catfish** production.

Support for Language Development

Name _____ Date _____

1. Write the letter of the picture and word that goes with the definition below.

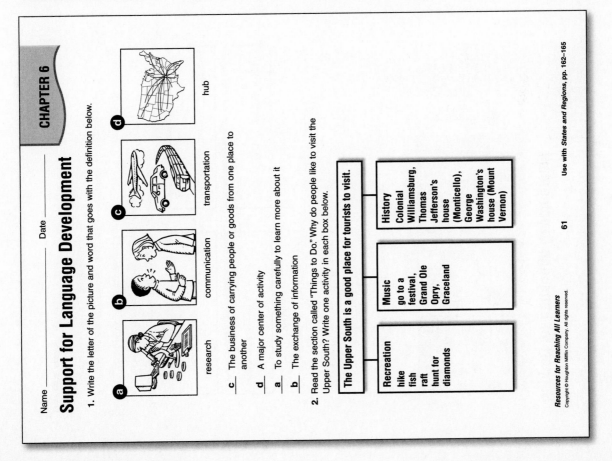

research   communication   transportation   hub

   c The business of carrying people or goods from one place to another

   d A major center of activity

   a To study something carefully to learn more about it

   b The exchange of information

2. Read the section called "Things to Do." Why do people like to visit the Upper South? Write one activity in each box below.

The Upper South is a good place for tourists to visit.

Recreation	Music	History
hike	go to a	Colonial
fish	festival,	Williamsburg,
raft	Grand Ole	Thomas
hunt for	Opry,	Jefferson's
diamonds	Graceland	house
		(Monticello),
		George
		Washington's
		house (Mount
		Vernon)

Answers *continued*

Name _____ Date _____

Support for Language Development

1. Write the letter of the word that goes with the definition below.

a demand   **b** supply

_b_ How much of a product producers will make at different prices

_a_ How much of a product consumers will buy at different prices

2. Complete the sentences to explain why the Midwest developed as it did.

Cause

The Midwest has rich **soil** and plenty of rainfall.

→

Effect

The Midwest became a major farming region.

3. Read "Supply and Demand" on page 199 of your textbook. Write the missing words in the sentences below.

A. Supply and **demand** affect each other.

B. As demand rises, the price tends to **rise**.

C. As supply rises, the price often **falls**.

Resources for Reaching All Learners
Copyright © Houghton Mifflin Company. All rights reserved.

64   Use with *States and Regions*, pp. 196–199

Name _____ Date _____

Support for Language Development

1. Write the letter of the picture and word that goes with the definition below.

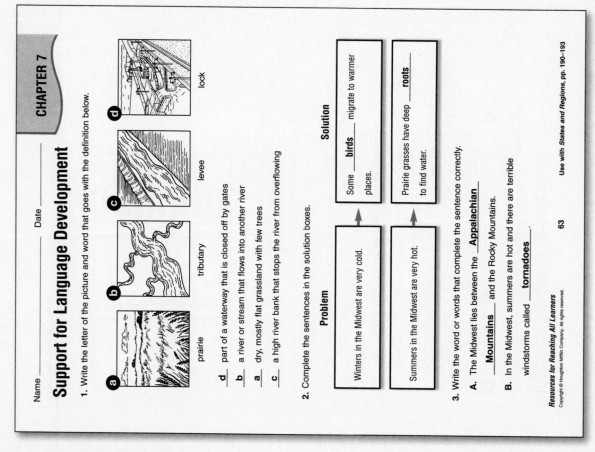

prairie   tributary   levee   lock

_d_ part of a waterway that is closed off by gates

_b_ a river or stream that flows into another river

_a_ dry, mostly flat grassland with few trees

_c_ a high river bank that stops the river from overflowing

2. Complete the sentences in the solution boxes.

Problem

Winters in the Midwest are very cold.

Solution

Some **birds** migrate to warmer places.

Problem

Summers in the Midwest are very hot.

Solution

Prairie grasses have deep **roots** to find water.

3. Write the word or words that complete the sentence correctly.

A. The Midwest lies between the **Appalachian Mountains** and the Rocky Mountains.

B. In the Midwest, summers are hot and there are terrible windstorms called **tornadoes**.

Resources for Reaching All Learners
Copyright © Houghton Mifflin Company. All rights reserved.

63   Use with *States and Regions*, pp. 190–193

Answers

Name _____ Date _____

Support for Language Development

1. Circle the word that goes with the definition.

a railway that runs above the ground on raised tracks — (elevated train)

elevation   chain   celebrated   train   elevator   (elevated train)

the payments for work — (wages)

wags   wedges   (wages)   warns

2. Read "Living in Chicago, Illinois" on page 219 of your textbook. Then write the word or words that complete the sentences correctly.

A. Chicago has **more** people than any other city in the Great Lakes States.

B. Chicago's location near important waterways helped it become a major **trading** center.

C. As Chicago grew, public **transportation** became necessary to take workers to and from downtown.

Name _____ Date _____

Support for Language Development

1. Write the letter of the word that goes with the definition below.

a homestead   b reservation   c assembly line

a a piece of land given to someone to settle and farm there

b land set aside by the government for American Indians

c a way of manufacturing goods where each worker does one small part of the job

2. Write the word or words that complete the sentence correctly.

A. Thomas Jefferson bought the **Louisiana** **Territory** from France in 1803.

B. Many **Germans** and **Scandinavians** immigrated to the Midwest.

C. The Homestead Act of 1862 gave land to people who would live there for **five** **years**.

Answers *continued*

Name _____ Date _____

Support for Language Development

1. Write in the letters that go with the definitions below.

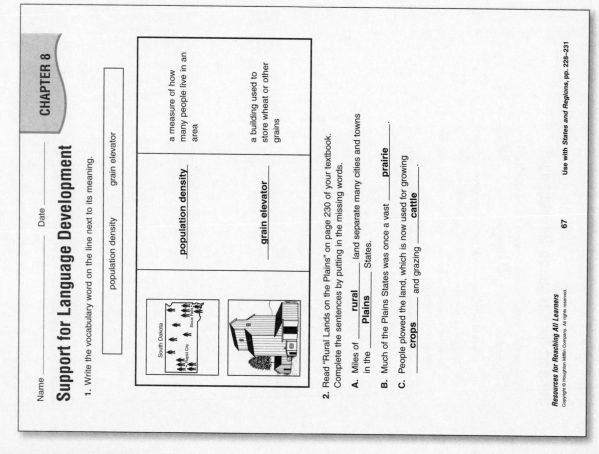

a — irrigation   b — hydroelectric power   c — arid

b electricity produced from flowing water

a a way of supplying land with water

c very dry

2. Read "Water, Climate, and Wildlife" on page 248 of your textbook. Then write the word or words that complete the sentence correctly.

A. The Pacific Ocean affects **climates** in the West.

B. Air from the Pacific gives the **northern** coast **more** rain than the southern coast.

C. The air stays dry as it flows down eastern mountains. This makes the climate there **arid** .

3. Read "Mountains in the West" on page 247 of your textbook. Draw a line from the landform to the word that tells how it was formed.

Rivers — Cascade Mountains
Tectonic plates — Rocky Mountains
Glaciers — Yosemite Valley
Volcanoes — Grand Canyon

Rocky Mountains
Cascade Mountains
Yosemite Valley
Grand Canyon

68   Use with *States and Regions*, pp. 246–249

Name _____ Date _____

Support for Language Development

1. Write the vocabulary word on the line next to its meaning.

population density   grain elevator

| **population density** | a measure of how many people live in an area |
| **grain elevator** | a building used to store wheat or other grains |

2. Read "Rural Lands on the Plains" on page 230 of your textbook. Complete the sentences by putting in the missing words.

A. Miles of **rural** land separate many cities and towns in the **Plains** States.

B. Much of the Plains States was once a vast **prairie** .

C. People plowed the land, which is now used for growing **crops** and grazing **cattle** .

67   Use with *States and Regions*, pp. 228–231

Answers

Support for Language Development

1. Write the vocabulary word on the line next to its meaning.

| mission | wagon train | transcontinental railroad |

transcontinental railroad	train system that linked the East and the West
mission	a settlement for teaching religion to local people
wagon train	a line of wagons that carried settlers and their belongings

2. Read "Spanish Settlements" on page 264 of your textbook. Fill in the missing words.

Causes

Spanish soldiers hoped to find gold.

As they moved into Indian land, they came into **conflict** with the Indians who lived there.

Effects

They traveled north and made a **settlement** at Santa Fe.

They used **force** to take Indian land.

Support for Language Development

1. Write in the letters of the picture that go with the definitions below.

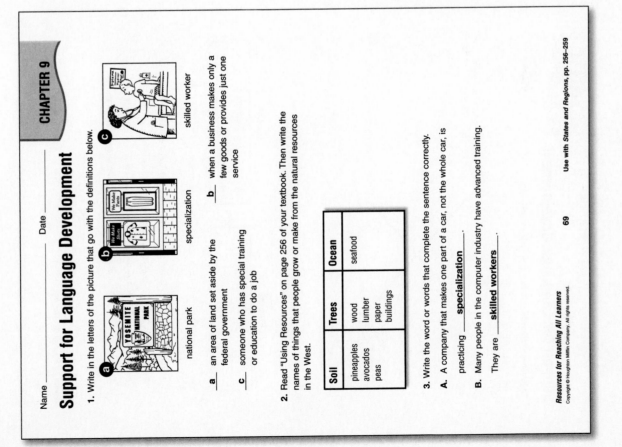

national park   specialization   skilled worker

a an area of land set aside by the federal government

b when a business makes only a few goods or provides just one service

c someone who has special training or education to do a job

2. Read "Using Resources" on page 256 of your textbook. Then write the names of things that people grow or make from the natural resources in the West.

Soil	Trees	Ocean
pineapples avocados peas	wood lumber paper buildings	seafood

3. Write the word or words that complete the sentence correctly.

A. A company that makes one part of a car, not the whole car, is practicing **specialization** .

B. Many people in the computer industry have advanced training. They are **skilled workers** .

Name ______________ Date ________ CHAPTER 10

Support for Language Development

1. Match each definition to its correct picture and word.

conservation — Using something carefully and not wasting it

weathering — The breakdown of rock caused by wind, water, and weather

2. Read the section of the lesson called "Using Water." Then read the sentences below. Use the correct words to complete the sentence.

Problem	Solution
There are only a few rivers. They are often overused.	Rivers have been **dammed** to create **reservoirs**.

3. Match the state on the left with a sentence that best describes it on the right.

- Arizona — The largest city in the Southwest is in this state.
- New Mexico — Most pueblos on the Rio Grande are in this state.
- Nevada — Some areas of this state only get 4 inches of rain a year.
- Utah — Tourists come to visit the natural arches in this state.

Resources for Reaching All Learners 71 Use with *States and Regions*, pp. 274–277

Name ______________ Date ________ CHAPTER 10

Support for Language Development

1. Write the letter of the picture and word that goes with the definition below.

a 
ecosystem

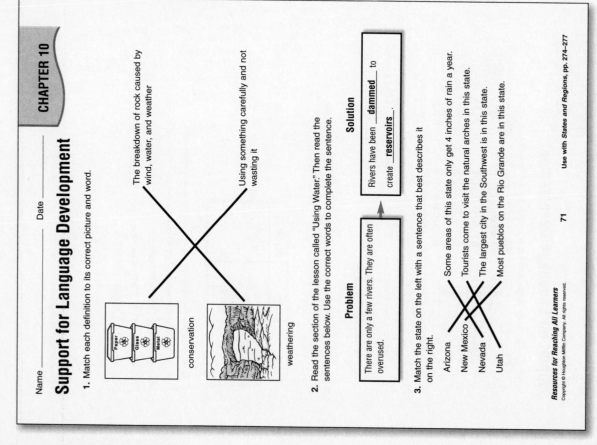

b 
habitat

c 
extinct

__a__ An environment and all its living things, working together as a unit

__c__ No longer existing

__b__ The natural home of a plant or animal

2. Read "Cities and Rural Areas." Then compare life in the urban and rural areas of the Mountain States. Use the phrases in the box to complete the diagram.

Urban	Both	Rural
many people; are centers of industry, entertainment, and health care	**enjoy outdoor activities**	**few people; raise sheep and cattle; travel to get supplies and services**

few people
enjoy outdoor activities
are centers of industry, entertainment, and health care
raise sheep and cattle
travel to get supplies and services
many people

Resources for Reaching All Learners 72 Use with *States and Regions*, pp. 282–285

Answers

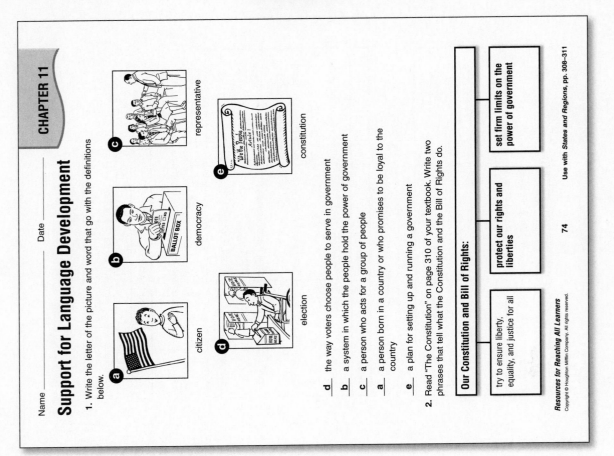

Name _____ Date _____

Support for Language Development

1. Write the letter of the picture and word that go with the definitions below.

a citizen
b democracy
c representative
d election
e constitution

__d__ the way voters choose people to serve in government

__b__ a system in which the people hold the power of government

__c__ a person who acts for a group of people

__a__ a person born in a country or who promises to be loyal to the country

__e__ a plan for setting up and running a government

2. Read "The Constitution" on page 310 of your textbook. Write two phrases that tell what the Constitution and the Bill of Rights do.

Our Constitution and Bill of Rights:

try to ensure liberty, equality, and justice for all	protect our rights and liberties	set firm limits on the power of government

Resources for Reaching All Learners
74 Use with *States and Regions*, pp. 308–311

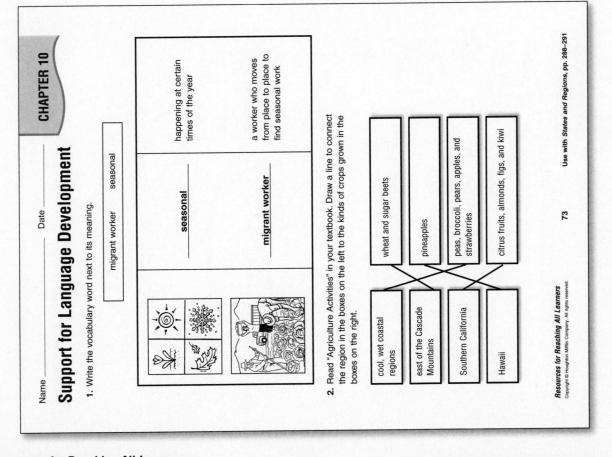

Name _____ Date _____

Support for Language Development

1. Write the vocabulary word next to its meaning.

migrant worker   seasonal

seasonal	happening at certain times of the year
migrant worker	a worker who moves from place to place to find seasonal work

2. Read "Agriculture Activities" in your textbook. Draw a line to connect the region in the boxes on the left to the kinds of crops grown in the boxes on the right.

cool, wet coastal regions

east of the Cascade Mountains

Southern California

Hawaii

wheat and sugar beets

pineapples

peas, broccoli, pears, apples, and strawberries

citrus fruits, almonds, figs, and kiwi

Resources for Reaching All Learners
73 Use with *States and Regions*, pp. 288–291

Answers *continued*

Name _____ Date _____

Support for Language Development

1. Write the vocabulary word on the line next to its meaning.

province	a unit of government into which a nation is divided

2. Canada and Mexico both border the United States, but they are very different. Fill in the chart with information about each country.

Feature	Canada	Mexico
Climate	frozen, cool, arctic	warm, can be cold in the mountains, dry
Mountain ranges	Rocky Mountains	Sierra Madre Occidental, Sierra Madre Oriental
Other landforms	Great Plains, Canadian Shield	Mexican Plateau, Baja California
Language	French, English	Spanish

3. Look at the map on page 321 of your textbook. Fill in the following chart with the names of the three largest countries in North America.

North America

United States	Mexico	Canada

Resources for Reaching All Learners
Copyright © Houghton Mifflin Company. All rights reserved.

76   Use with *States and Regions*, pp. 320–323

Name _____ Date _____

Support for Language Development

1. Write the letter of the word that goes with the definition below.

a interdependence   **b** prosperity   **c** heritage   **d** volunteer

d   someone who agrees to provide a service without pay

a   a relationship in which people depend on each other

c   traditions that people have honored for many years

b   wealth and success

2. Read "Linking Regions" on page 314 of your textbook. The United States is linked by several communications systems. Find some examples in the text or think of others. Write their names in the small ovals.

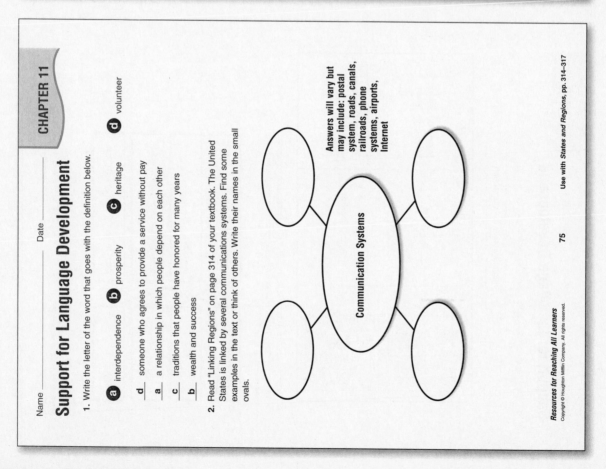

Communication Systems

Answers will vary but may include: postal system, roads, canals, railroads, phone systems, airports, Internet

Resources for Reaching All Learners
Copyright © Houghton Mifflin Company. All rights reserved.

75   Use with *States and Regions*, pp. 314–317

Answers

Name _____ Date _____

Support for Language Development

1. Circle the word that goes with the definition.

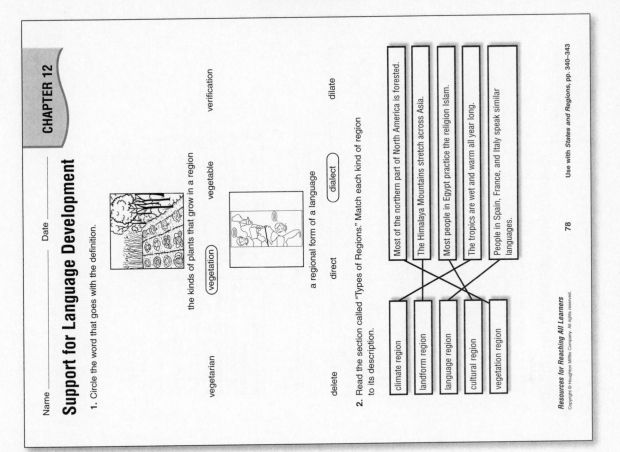

the kinds of plants that grow in a region

vegetarian   (vegetation)   vegetable   verification

a regional form of a language

delete   direct   (dialect)   dilate

2. Read the section called "Types of Regions." Match each kind of region to its description.

climate region	Most of the northern part of North America is forested.
landform region	The Himalaya Mountains stretch across Asia.
language region	Most people in Egypt practice the religion Islam.
cultural region	The tropics are wet and warm all year long.
vegetation region	People in Spain, France, and Italy speak similar languages.

78   Use with *States and Regions*, pp. 340–343

Name _____ Date _____

Support for Language Development

1. Write the vocabulary word on the line next to its meaning.

rain forest   isthmus

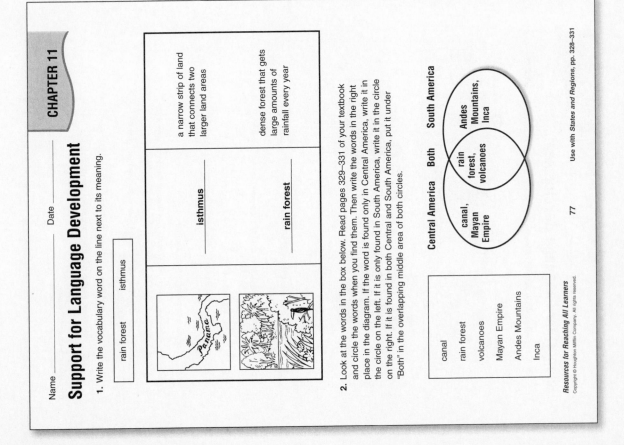

isthmus — a narrow strip of land that connects two larger land areas

rain forest — dense forest that gets large amounts of rainfall every year

2. Look at the words in the box below. Read pages 329–331 of your textbook and circle the words when you find them. Then write the words in the right place in the diagram. If the word is found only in Central America, write it in the circle on the left. If it is only found in South America, write it in the circle on the right. If it is found in both Central and South America, put it under "Both" in the overlapping middle area of both circles.

canal
rain forest
volcanoes
Mayan Empire
Andes Mountains
Inca

Central America   **Both**   **South America**

canal, Mayan Empire

rain forest, volcanoes

Andes Mountains, Inca

77   Use with *States and Regions*, pp. 328–331

Answers *continued*

Name _____ Date _____

Support for Language Development

1. Write the vocabulary word on the line next to its meaning.

nongovernmental organization	a group that is not part of a national government
international law	a set of basic rules to which the United States and many other countries have agreed

2. Read the section called "The United Nations" in your textbook. Draw a line to connect the name of the UN organization or document to what it does.

The World Health Organization — helps countries build their economies.

The Universal Declaration of Human Rights — helps improve health conditions around the world.

The World Bank — protects the basic rights of people in all countries.

Name _____ Date _____

Support for Language Development

1. Write the letter of the picture and word that goes with each definition below.

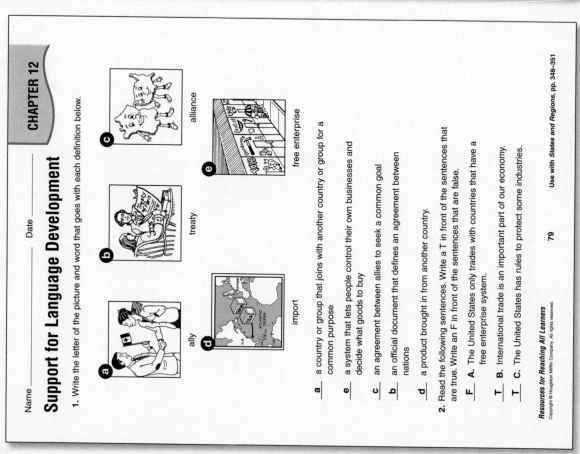

a — ally b — treaty c — alliance d — import e — free enterprise

a a country or group that joins with another country or group for a common purpose

e a system that lets people control their own businesses and decide what goods to buy

c an agreement between allies to seek a common goal

b an official document that defines an agreement between nations

d a product brought in from another country.

2. Read the following sentences. Write a T in front of the sentences that are true. Write an F in front of the sentences that are false.

F A. The United States only trades with countries that have a free enterprise system.

T B. International trade is an important part of our economy.

T C. The United States has rules to protect some industries.